Zebra Finches

ZEBRA FINCHES

by
Cyril H. Rogers

The Bird Keeper's Library

Series Editor
DENNIS KELSEY-WOOD

K·R Books Ltd, Edlington, Horncastle, Lincs

© K & R Books Ltd

First published 1979 by
K & R Books Ltd, Edlington Hall,
Edlington, Horncastle, Lincs

ISBN 0 903264 19 6

Printed in Grt Britain by R. & R. Clark Ltd of Edinburgh and bound by Hunter & Foulis Ltd, also of Edinburgh Typeset by Woolaston Parker Ltd of Leicester

CONTENTS

ACKNOWLEDGEMENTS

The publishers of this book would like to express their thanks to the following people without whom this work would not have been possible. Harry Lacey for his superb photography, Thomas Brosset of Sweden for his additional photography and the Zebra Finch Society, in particular B. C. E. Binns and J. A. W. Prior who made available the fine colour portraits of the various varieties.

Carol Robertson for her proof-reading and finally Cyril Rogers who, as always, can be relied upon to provide a comprehensive and enjoyable manuscript.

LIST OF ILLUSTRATIONS

Endpapers: (left to right) Fawn hen, Penguin hen, Grey Hen, Silver cock, Grey cock, Penguin cock, Silver hen, Fawn cock.

LINE ILLUSTRATIONS

COLOUR PLATES

Chapter 1

HISTORY

Wild type Zebra Finches

The wild Zebra Finches (*Taeniopygia guttata casta-notis*) are to be found in large flocks widely distributed over Australia and some nearby islands. They live and breed in areas where water is available near large grass covered plains and low scrublands. Records do not give exact dates when Zebra Finches were first imported into Great Britain and Europe, being only briefly mentioned by Ornithologists of the day. It is thought that during the early part of the eighteen hundreds Zebra Finches must have been amongst the many species of Australian birds that were brought into the old world. However, my friend, C.af Enehjelm, one time Curator of the Zoological Gardens at Helsingfors, Finland, now living in Denmark, throws some light on the early days of the Zebra Finch in his excellent article "History of the Zebra Finch" which appears in the 1961 edition of The Zebra Finch Society's Year Book. The following are extracts from that article—

"Already prior to his first journey to Australia in 1838 John Gould gave a description of the Zebra Finch. The bird was, however, described earlier. The French naturalist L. J. P. Viellot (1748–1831) in his wonderful book 'Histoire naturelle des plus beaux oiseaux chanteurs de zone torride' (1805–?) gives a rather correct description of the bird which he calls Le Bengali mouchete, however, with the wrong statement that it originates from the Moluccans. This is probably the first description of the species, but it is a question, if the birds described did not belong to the island species from Timor and Flores. It is more than probable, if Monsieur Viellot himself ever possessed living specimens. . . .

There are no statements when or by whom the Zebra Finch was first brought alive to Europe, nor any account about the first breeding in captivity. Certainly Dr. Karl Russ, the grand old man of the German aviculture, states in some editions of his books, that the bird was already bred by Viellot, which Karl Neunzig repeats in later editions of the books, edited by him. ('Schon von Viellot gezuchter.') It seems, however, that Dr. Russ was not quite sure about this point. In the first edition of his 'Prachtfinken' (The Weaver Finches) 1879 he writes 'Viellot has bred this bird and also gives a picture of the juvenile plumage. If this bird, however, is identical with Bengali mouchete, and if the Moluccan Islands only wrongly stated as the country of origin, I have not been able to confirm.' . . .

It will therefore hardly ever be solved when or by whom the Zebra Finch was first bred in captivity. No doubt, however, this happened at a comparatively early date. In the first volume of the German paper 'Die gefiederte Welt' (The Feathered World) 1872 the breeding of Zebra Finches is already considered quite common and in the first edition of his earlier mentioned book 'Die Prachtfinken' Dr. Russ writes that 'that the experiences from the breeding of Zebra Finches are fundamental for all breeding of cage birds.' In the first edition of Dr. Bechstein's 'Naturgeschichte der Stubenvogel' (1794) the Zebra Finch is not mentioned neither in later editions. . . . "

According to that great Ornithologist the late Allen Silver the first book published in the English language on Foreign Birds to have a full account of the Zebra Finch was *Foreign Cage Birds* by C. W. Gedney and issued in 1879.

Undoubtedly aviculturists quickly discovered that these vivacious little birds were very hardy and could be induced to breed quite freely under captive conditions. For many years the main supply of Zebra Finches came from birds trapped and exported from Australia supplemented to some extent by European aviary bred stock. The few birds from British aviaries were mostly surplus from strains that were used principally to rear more rare Foreign species. By the beginning of this present century Zebra Finches were being bred in cage and aviary in quite considerable numbers by Foreign Bird keepers in many countries.

When a cock Normal Grey Zebra Finch is examined it will clearly be seen from whence their present day name was derived. The clearly defined fine black marking on a white ground from chin to chest bar is strongly reminiscent of the markings of the Zebra. Although these birds are now universally called Zebra Finches they are still known to some older aviculturists by their old name—Chestnut Eared Finches. Here again it is a good descriptive name as the Normal Grey (and some of the other colour mutations) cocks have distinctive rich chestnut coloured ear patches.

That most useful book by Neville W. Cayley, F.R.Z.S. *Australian Finches in Bush and Aviary* gives information on some seven different sub species of Zebra Finches that are to be found in various districts of Australia. In *Birds of Western Australia*, Third edition, by D. L. Serventy and H. M. Whittell, there are details of no less than eleven sub species. In the Island of Timor there is at least one more species of Zebra Finch.

As it is with other species that have numerous sub species the differences between them are only slight and the various sub species will interbreed quite freely in captivity and in the wild where their territory overlaps. The differences are to be found in the depth and distribution of colours and size, which although quite small can be seen clearly. Without a doubt the consignments of wild caught Zebra Finches that were at one time imported into Great Britain and Europe must have contained examples of most of the sub species. All these undoubtedly have been in the foundation stock of the domesticated Zebra Finches and this accounts for the slight variations in shades of colour, size, and shape of our present day strains of Zebra Finches and their mutations.

When conditions had settled down after the second world war and the breeding of birds had started again in earnest the various strains of Zebra Finches breeding in cages and aviaries began to produce more mutant colour forms. It will be seen from the following Chapters on the individual mutations how each one has been developed and true breeding forms established. Immediately domesticated cage birds begin to have new colour forms the interest of breeders in that species inevitably rises dramatically. This was certainly the case with Zebra Finches and their breeding, development, and exhibiting, began to increase world wide. This rise in popularity encouraged a small group of British Zebra Finch enthusiasts to meet and form The Zebra Finch Society to cater especially for this species and its mutations. From a small beginning The Zebra Finch Society has now become an important and influential Specialist Society with Area Societies covering the Country. There are also large numbers of local Cage Bird Societies and some Overseas Societies that

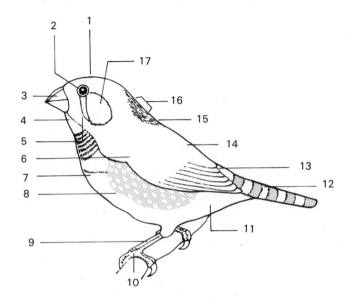

AREAS OF A ZEBRA FINCH

1 Crown
2 Eye
3 Beak
4 Throat
5 Tear Mark
6 Wing Butt
7 Chest Bar
8 Flanking
9 Shank

10 Feet
11 Vent
12 Tail Barring
13 Flights
14 Back (saddle)
15 Back
16 Neck
17 Ear Lobe

are affiliated to the Parent Body and governed by its exhibition rules.

Until the formation of The Zebra Finch Society in 1952 Zebra Finches were looked upon as attractive small Foreign Birds and were treated as such at exhibitions. The Society changed this image as in 1958 they declared Zebra Finches and all their mutations to be a thoroughly domesticated species and no longer to be classed as Foreign Birds. This decision was quickly accepted by the Cage Bird Fancy in Great Britain and most other countries in the world where these delightful little birds are bred. The Zebra Finch Society has helped to develop the various colour mutations and evolved standards of perfection for each recognised new form, and this has put Zebra Finches firmly in the picture as domesticated cage and aviary birds. At some of the exhibitions in recent years several hundreds of pairs of the various colours of Zebra Finches have been shown.

Chapter 2

NORMAL GREY ZEBRA FINCHES

The breeding of Zebra Finches in their original colouring is still extremely popular amongst fanciers in spite of the attractions offered by some of the new colour mutations. Normal Grey Zebra Finches are used extensively to improve and develop the new colours and to some extent this procedure has been detrimental to the colour itself. Because of this cross pairing which of course has been essential it is difficult to find many strains of pure unmixed Normal Grey Zebra Finches although there are still a few breeders who maintain pure studs.

Sometimes the result of crossing Normal Grey Zebra Finches with other colours can be seen by the deterioration of the purity of the grey colouring, principally on the wings where it shows as light edging to the feathers, and brownish tinting. Other evidence can be observed by ticks of white on head, neck or back, and the odd white flight feather or two. In addition to the colour faults caused by crossing pairing there can be slight differences in overall depth of shade and also individual areas of colour due to the blending of the various sub species in the creation of our present day domesticated birds. Some specimens of Normal Greys are very dark and have correspondingly deeply coloured chestnut ear lobes and flankings whereas others are quite pale, with the majority being medium grey in colour. When selecting pairs for breeding or exhibiting the owners should always try to match each pair for colour, substance and cobby type. When a breeder knows the potential of the stock the selection of the breeding partners will depend on the careful balancing of each bird's qualities.

If a breeder wants to develop a strain of good type Normal Grey Zebra Finches I would suggest that a start be made with no less than three unrelated pairs, each bird selected for its correctness of colour, type and substance. Such birds should be as free as possible from other colour characters in their genetical makeup. When two Normal Grey Zebra Finches are mated together they should if pure produce only young of their colour. However, a considerable number of Normal Greys have been used for cross breeding and consequently can carry hidden in their makeup characters for other colours. These characters can be Recessive or Sex-linked ones, and with the former they will not be revealed unless two compatible characters happen to come together. A typical example of this is Normal Grey/White to Normal Grey/White which gives the theoretical expectation of 25% White, 50% Normal Grey/White and 25% Normal Grey. This means that an average of three out of four young will be grey in colour with only one being pure grey, the other two carry the white character. When a pure Grey is paired to one that is "split" for White half of their young will also be "splits". Unfortunately there is no way of identifying the pure birds from the ones that are "split" except by test pairings. This being so the "split" colour can be passed on unseen for many generations and then suddenly appear in what was thought to be a pure strain.

In the evolution of a pure strain of Greys any other colours that appear should be excluded from that strain together with the parents of the birds that were produced. By this method of selection a good, sound, pure breeding stock can be built up and this is applicable to all the colours. From time to time specimens of pure Normal Greys will be needed to strengthen or improve the newer colour mutations. These crossbred Normal Greys should be used solely for the purpose for which they were bred and excluded from pure Normal Grey strains. There is a great advantage in having known pure Normal Greys as it is much simpler to select matched exhibition pairs from them because of their physical likeness and matching colour and pattern. When it comes to test pairings pure Normal Greys form a solid base on which to construct experimental breeding. In fact if the genetical makeup of any birds used in experimental work is not known findings can be incorrect and misleading.

Normal Grey Zebra Finches behave in a Dominant manner to all other colour mutations and therefore these birds can carry in "split" form other colour characters. There is however one Dominant character that can alter the shade of the Normal Greys (and all other colours) and that is the Dominant Dilute character. The addition of one or two Dominant Dilute characters to the genetical makeup of Normal Greys produces birds that are still basically grey but of a diluted tone of colour. (See Chapters 7 and 8.)

Colour description

COCK. Eyes dark (shades of dark red or brown). Beak coral red. Feet and legs pink, red or reddish brown. Head dark grey with some darker ticking to centre of head. Neck, back and wings grey. Chest bar black. Throat and upper breast above bar black zebra lines on a white ground running from check to cheek. Tear

marks black. Cheek lobes deep reddish orange. Underparts below bar white with some slight fawnish tinting
in vent area. Tail black with white barrings, side
flankings rich reddish brown ornamented with many
small white spots.

HEN. As other hens to match cock. Beak paler red.

Show colour faults: Light edges to wing feathers, irregular
chest bar, too narrow or poorly spotted flankings and
blotchy overall colouring. Indistinct tear mark. Traces
of chest barring on hens.

Grey cock Zebra Finch giving alarm call.

Chapter 3

WHITE ZEBRA FINCHES

It would seem that the Whites are the oldest mutation
that has been noticed by aviculturists. In the early
days of keeping small Australian birds in captivity in
many countries it is very possible that colour mutations
other than White (or Pied) may have occurred and
passed unnoticed. White birds on the other hand would
have been seen immediately they appeared even in a
large mixed collection of Exotics, and before the turn of
the first quarter of this century White Zebra Finches
actually appeared. It was in a mixed aviary of an
Australian breeder, A. J. Woods of Sydney, that the
first known Whites were bred during 1921. Being a
Recessive mutation they naturally took slightly longer
to establish than the Sex-linked Chestnut-flanked
Whites and Albinos. The Australian White strain was
established and examples quickly spread to other parts
of the world. It is thought that the White strains of
Zebra Finches now existing in Great Britain were
founded on examples of the original mutation. Further
White mutations may well have occurred in various
places but being of the same hereditary nature as the
originals passed unnoticed. It is always possible for the
same mutation to occur again in any flock of birds and
unless it had a different hereditary makeup it would not
be recognised as a new mutation. White Zebra Finches
are always attractive in a mixed coloured collection
and are considered most pleasing as exhibition birds.
In actual fact a pair of White Zebra Finches bred and

A balanced pair of good pure coloured White Zebra Finches.

exhibited by Len Harris of Birmingham were the first of their species to win the Supreme Award for Best Birds in Show at the National Exhibition of Cage and Aviary Birds at Alexandra Palace, London in 1972. This great success did much to boost Zebra Finches as exhibition birds and I shall always be proud to have been one of the four Judges who made this historic award.

It will be realised that for exhibition purposes both members of matched pairs must be pure white in colour and quite free from the slightest trace of dark flecking. Such birds can of course only be consistently produced through the careful selection by the owner of each breeding pair of birds. As with all species of exhibition birds type and overall good quality can only be improved and successfully maintained by the outcrossing method with other colours that have the required features in their genetical makeup. Breeders of Whites have been experimenting with different colour outcrosses for years and many have found that the purest coloured Whites are derived from the use of the Fawn mutation as an outcross. Up to the appearance of the Fawns in 1927 and for some years after the vast majority of Whites showed some grey flecking to a greater or lesser extent. Whites masking Fawn (Fawn Whites) can still show some flecking which is pale fawn in colour and consequently not so prominent as it is when it is grey. The careful selection of the most lightly marked birds for several generations of breeding is the secret of the successful production of pure coloured Whites. Normal Greys and Normal Grey Pieds have together with most other colours been used as outcrosses for Whites, and of course some of these have resulted in good quality White birds. On the other hand the use of Fawns as outcrosses have produced better quality and purer Whites than the other colours.

Colour description

COCK AND HEN. Eyes dark (brown or red). Feet and legs pink or reddish pink. Pure white all through. Hens mostly have beaks that are a paler shade of red.
Show colour faults: Flecking of dark colouring on neck, mantle and upper wings.

Chapter 4

ALBINO ZEBRA FINCHES

With all domesticated species of birds it is only a question of time before an Albino (or Lutino) mutation appears and Zebra Finches have adhered to this pattern. Although Albino Zebra Finches have been bred in Great Britain in small numbers since the late 1950s they have not yet been fully established or recognised. In Australia however Albinos are quite widely bred and have separate classes at bird exhibitions. The exact date of their appearance I have not yet been able to track down but it seems it was well before the British mutation.

Albinos differ in two respects from the normal Whites and are visually identified by the colour of their eyes. The eyes of all other Zebra Finch mutations have a dark iris which is surrounded by an iris ring of varying shades of solid red or brown. With the Albinos the eyes are bright red all through like those seen in the Lutino Greenfinch. Their colour is pure clear white without any sign of flecking which of course can also be said for many first rate exhibition Normal Whites. However, if Albino Zebra Finches are produced their plumage will always be clear white. The beaks of both cocks and hens are exactly like those of the Normal Whites, being deep coral red in the cocks and a shade or two paler in the hens.

Their method of reproduction is sex-linked exactly like the Fawn and Chestnut-flanked White mutations, and examples of these can be found in Chapter 17. The only examples I have seen have been hens and I was particularly struck by the bright pinkness of their feet and legs making them look very fragile. I would think that at some future date it will be found that the best Albinos from an exhibition angle will be those masking Fawn. It has been found with the normal Whites that the Fawn forms are invariably the purest in colour and undoubtedly the best for feather quality.

Albinos have also been reported as appearing in India amongst a flock of mixed colours all cross pairing and breeding together for a number of years. In an aviary of this type it is certain that close inbreeding will take place and this may have resulted in the Albinos turning up. Although I have no definite proof that these birds were actually Albinos I think they may well have been. It was said that these red-eyed Whites were rather weakly, many dying before leaving their nests, and were noticeably smaller than the normally coloured birds of the flock. Similarly red-eyed White birds have been seen in European aviaries but again do not seem to have been established.

Colour description

COCK AND HEN. Eyes clear red. Beak coral red in cock and a slightly less deep shade in hen. Feet and legs bright flesh pink. Colour pure white throughout.
There are no colour faults in Albinos.

Chapter 5

CHESTNUT-FLANKED WHITE ZEBRA FINCHES

The first known Chestnut-flanked Whites appeared about 1937 in Queensland, Australia, amongst wild flocks from which they were trapped and taken into breeding aviaries. By careful breeding this mutation was quickly developed and in due course specimens were exported to various parts of the world. Originally they were known in Australia as Marked Whites which of course they are but later the mutation was to become known universally as Chestnut-flanked White emphasising the prominent feature of the colouring carried by the cock birds. This was sound reasoning and the name Chestnut-flanked White was adopted as "Marked White" could equally apply to badly flecked ordinary Whites and the Saddle-backed Whites. A further name used in Europe is Masked White and this is because the majority of young nest feather birds show a considerable amount of blackish feathering on their heads and faces. Again this name is not good and is only descriptive of immature specimens. Marmosette is a further name that was used for a time by some European breeders and bird dealers and will occasionally be heard mentioned in European articles. After this spate of names the mutation has now settled down to be known world wide as Chestnut-flanked White.

In the early days of their production it was quickly discovered that the Chestnut-flanked White mutation followed the same manner of inheritance as the Fawns and they were the second Sex-linked variety to appear.

There can be Chestnut-flanked forms of all other mutations but the best coloured specimens are evolved from the Normal Grey and Fawn kinds. Such birds as Chestnut-flanked White Pieds or Chestnut-flanked White Penguins, although interesting examples of breeders' skill, are not particularly striking colour-wise and do not appeal much to exhibitors. The White form of the Chestnut-flanked White is of course identical in colouring to their ordinary White fore-bears as the White mutation masks all other colours.

As with all livestock different breeders have their own particular method which they think will give the best coloured stock. I would advise any breeder who has found certain matings amongst the stock to continue with such matings and not be put off with other sug-gested crosses. It seems to be agreed quite generally that good evenly coloured Normal Greys are the best out-cross for improving the overall colour of the Chestnut-flanked Whites ultimately bred. At the same time it is most important that the Chestnut-flanked Whites used are most carefully selected for their depth of markings and pureness of their white ground colour. Being a sex-linked variety the sex of the Normal Greys used for outcrossing will have a definite effect on the actual colouring of the young produced. If Normal Grey cocks are mated with Chestnut-flanked White hens the resulting young will be either pure Normal Grey hens or Normal Grey/Chestnut-flanked White cocks. The reverse cross of Chestnut-flanked White cocks to Normal Grey hens will give all pure Chestnut-flanked White hens and all Normal Grey/Chestnut-flanked White cocks. A Normal/Chestnut-flanked White cock paired to a Normal Grey hen will give a percentage of Chestnut-flanked White hens but cock birds of this colouring cannot appear until a Chestnut-flanked

White or a "split" Chestnut-flanked White cock is mated to a Chestnut-flanked White hen so that both members of the pair actually have the character in their genetical makeup. In fact Chestnut-flanked Whites follow the same pattern of inheritance as do all Sex-linked colour mutations, see Chapter 17 for diagrams.

By using selected pairs for breeding and not only incorporating colour but also type, substance and feather quality a steady improvement in the overall standard of the stock can be maintained. One point I would like to make here is that in recent years it has been noticed that often amongst the boldest specimens of Chestnut-flanked Whites their ground colour has become very strongly suffused with a cream shade. It would appear that both the white ground and the newer creamy ground are in existence and may well appear from the same pairings. I have looked closely into this and find that there is strong evidence that these creamy shaded birds are a further mutation of the same kind of character. We know that this is a possibility as it has occurred with other kinds of birds and the two or more mutations will interbreed quite normally. I make this point as there are often strong arguments why in recent years there has been an apparent deterioration in the colouring of Chestnut-flanked Whites. It has also been noted that there can be a very big variation in the colour of the cheek patches, flankings and chest markings of the cock birds. When selecting pairs for both breeding and exhibiting the finer points of purity of ground colour together with depth and clarity of markings on hens as well as cocks should be observed.

The visual difference in the colouring of normal White (including all White forms) and Chestnut-flanked White cocks is clear to see but with hens it is not always so. White hens may show flecking on head, neck or back, or on all three of these areas, however with Chestnut-flanked White hens fleck markings are only present on top of head and never on neck or back. The important distinguishing feature with Chestnut-flanked White hens is they always have tear marks and tail barring, both of these are absent in Normal Whites. Even with young birds in nest feather these colour differences are quite apparent.

Whilst on the subject of hens I must mention about head fleck markings on Chestnut-flanked Whites which some breeders have been trying to eliminate from their strains. These markings are part of the original pattern of this mutation and are permissible in exhibition birds. It has been noted that if these particular markings are reduced by selective pairings a corresponding reduction is seen with all markings on both cocks and hens. Ideal pairs of birds should have the characteristic markings as deep as possible on a ground as clear white as possible.

Colour description
COCK. Eyes dark (shades of dark red or brown). Beak coral red. Feet and legs pink. Head, neck, back and wings as white as possible. Underparts pure white. Breast bar as near black as possible. Tear markings same shade as breast bar. Cheek lobes orange. Tail white with barring to match breast barring. Flank markings reddish brown with clear white even spots.
HEN. As other hens to match cock. May have light markings on head.

Show colour faults: The main fault is heavy cream suffusion on both sexes. Lack of depth of characteristic markings on cocks and indistinct tear and tail markings on hens. Traces of chest barring on hens.

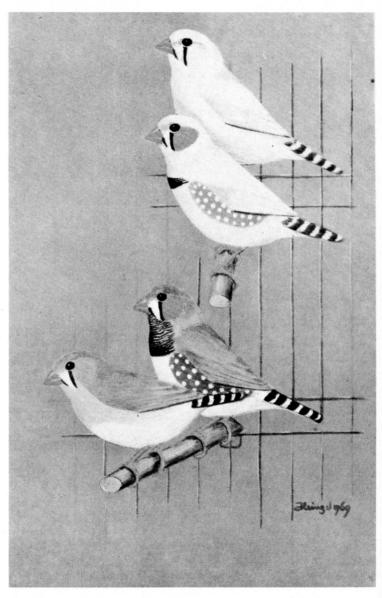

1. A pair of Chestnut-Flanked Whites and a pair of Fawns.

Chapter 6

FAWN ZEBRA FINCHES

It is mentioned in some of the older books on cage and aviary birds that there were certain colour varieties bred amongst flocks of Zebra Finches in aviaries. No details are given about these birds and their difference in colouring may have been just those found in the wild sub species of the Grey Zebra Finch flying in Australia. On the other hand it could well have been Cinnamon (Fawn) as this colour change is often the first mutation to appear in a species either in the wild or in breeding aviaries. It was at one time thought that Cinnamons (Fawns) originated in South Africa but on investigation it appears that the South African birds were in fact from stock obtained from Australia. The first Fawns were bred and established in 1927 and for a number of years were confined to Australian collections.

In the magazine of the Foreign Bird League Vol. 33 No. 5 September/October 1967 there is a reprint of an article that first appeared in the Avicultural Society of Australia's magazine of August 1958 on the "Origin of the Fawn Zebra Finch". The following extract from that article will, I feel sure, clear up the speculation about the first Fawn Zebra Finches—

" . . . the original birds were observed in a locality well outside the general rainfall area where there is a lack of vegetation so abundant in the higher rainfall areas. These conditions rarely vary from one year to another—with possibly one good rain season in five. One compensating factor in the area is a permanent spring which ensures a constant supply of water. Apart from this, the country is distinctly arid and, as would be imagined, the day temperatures are high.

However, at night, temperatures usually drop considerably and, consequently, early morning temperatures are also very low. The camp fire is therefore a prominent feature in the life of the outback residents and, around these, centres the initial story of the origin of the Fawn Zebra.

The original birds were two sports of a fawn mutation, and were observed flying around with a very large flock of normal Grey Zebras. In seeking warmth, these birds with their normal coloured grey mates, would venture close to the hot coals and ashes of the dying fire on cold mornings. Many hundreds of these birds were trapped over and over again, until the two sports were finally caught. The two birds were hens and both were of the fawn mutation, carrying the markings of the true fawn of to-day. Having been trapped, they were promptly dispatched to Adelaide and the slow and tedious task of breeding progeny similar to that of the two birds trapped was begun.

For several years, all the abnormal birds bred were hens and were not fawns. They were a poor blotchy silver and, when eventually the first males were bred, they carried very little colour in their ear patches. Being of this colour, these birds in many instances were referred to as "Smokies". Upholding their reputation, these birds soon produced quite a little colony and as their numbers were a little high for Mr. Fred Lewitzka to handle, some were farmed out to fanciers who made good use of them. . . . "

The first specimens of this mutation that appeared in Great Britain were commonly called Cinnamons and in the 1953 Year Book of the Zebra Finch Society both Fawns and Cinnamons were quoted as varieties. I saw examples of both the Fawns and Cinnamons and came to the conclusion that the darker coloured birds were being called Cinnamons and the paler kind Fawns although undoubtedly they were members of the same mutation. To overcome possible breeding and exhibition confusion it was decided by The Zebra Finch Society that the name Fawn should be used for this mutation and this was universally approved. Generally speaking the name Cinnamon is used in the bird world to indicate that the mutation is on a yellow ground whereas Fawn is used to describe white ground birds.

I said in the Chapter on the Normal Grey Zebra Finch that there were numerous sub species in the wild and that they varied a little in their colour distribution and shade and their size. In addition to the clearly recognisable light and dark forms of the Fawn there are other colour phases comparable with the variations as seen in Normal Greys. This fact makes it more difficult to match pairs for exhibition where it is essential that both members of a pair should show the same shade and depth of colouring. When selecting pairs for show the operation should be done in a good natural light to ensure that birds of the correct shades are put together. Artificial light causes the colours of all Zebra Finches to appear different from when seen in a clear natural light. Matched exhibition pairs invariably make good pairs for breeding as such pairs mostly give a much more evenly coloured result than if they had been mated haphazardly.

The best evenly coloured Fawns are invariably produced by Fawn to Fawn pairing with each member of a pair being carefully selected for purity of colour shade, substance and cobby type. From time to time improvements in a strain of Fawns may be needed and it is generally thought that selected Normal Greys are the best birds for the purpose. When Normal Fawn pairings are made only good quality evenly coloured birds should be used otherwise the colour of the resulting Fawns may be spoiled. As the Fawn mutation is a sex-linked one the sex of the birds used for outcrossing will have an immediate result on the colour of the first cross young. Normal Grey cocks paired to Fawn hens will produce all normally coloured young with the cocks being carriers of Fawn or Normal Grey/Fawns as they are mostly known. The Normal Grey hens from these matings will be pure Normal Grey and exactly the same genetically as Normal Greys bred from two pure Normal Greys. It is only the cock birds that actually carry the Fawn character. When the pairings are reversed and Fawn cocks are mated to Normal Grey hens all the young cocks are again Normal Grey/ Fawns but all the young hens are pure Fawns. If any other colours should appear from such crosses then the parent birds are carriers of these colours. As an example, if Whites appear in the nest then both parents must be "split" for White or if Chestnut-flanked White hens turn up the cock parent must be "split" for that character.

Normal Grey/Fawn cocks paired to Normal Grey hens give the theoretical expectations of 25% Normal Grey/Fawn cocks, 25% pure Fawn hens and 50% Normal Grey cocks and hens. Breeders have often found that such crosses are a good way of producing first class Fawn hens for the eventual use as mates for either Normal Grey/Fawn or Fawn cocks. Fawn cocks can only result from two kinds of matings—Fawn cocks to Fawn hens and "split" Fawn cocks to Fawn hens. It is this latter mating that is most frequently used when developing a strain of first class Fawns. The theoretical expectation from pairing "split" Fawn cocks to Fawn hens is 25 % Fawn cocks, 25 % Fawn hens, 25 % "split" Fawn cocks and 25 % Normal Grey hens. It must always be realised that in single pairings of any kind the numbers of each colour may vary although when a number of results are taken collectively the percentages will be found to work out correctly.

In previous paragraphs I have shown how good Fawn hens and Normal Grey/Fawn cocks can be bred to provide the breeder with sound material for the cross pairing just quoted. When matching up the pairs not only has colour to be considered but also substance, type, feather quality and breeding performance must be included. Although these points have to be considered with all matings it is the initial ones that have the greatest bearing in the establishment of a really first rate strain of Fawns. It will be realised that Fawn hens can be bred from the crossing of many different colours providing the cocks are carriers of the Fawn character. Many of these birds are excellent material for strengthening and also for outcrossing when new blood or special features are desired in a strain. Fawns themselves are of great value to use in the building up of the less popular mutations as the majority of them are fine quality birds and have excellent feather and type which are essential in developing newer varieties.

Colour description

COCK. Eyes dark (dark red or brown). Beak coral red. Feet and legs deep pink. Head, neck and wings even fawn (light or dark). Breast bar black. Throat and upper breast fawn with zebra lines running from cheek to cheek and continuing down to breast bar. Underparts white, cheek lobes orange, tail dark barred with white. Side flankings reddish brown with clear even white spots.

HEN. As other hens but of the same shade of fawn as the cocks. Beak paler red.

Show colour faults: Light shading on wings and mantle and light tips to secondary flights. Uneven or broken chest bars and poorly spotted flankings. Indistinct tear marks. Variation in depth and tone of colour between cock and hen of pairs. Traces of chest barring on hens.

Chapter 7

SILVER ZEBRA FINCHES

Dominant Silver Zebra Finches

Amongst most races of domesticated cage and aviary birds mutations occur which do not actually change a colour but alter its depth of shade. With Zebra Finches such a mutation has appeared in both Recessive and Dominant breeding forms and has produced some beautiful and interesting shades of the existing colours. Exact information on the breeding of the first Dominant Dilutes appears to be somewhat sketchy and the presence of the Recessive form which appeared at approximately the same time has no doubt confused the issue. Nevertheless it is a very strong possibility that their native Australia was again the home of the original mutation. It is also difficult to ascertain which came first—the Dominant Dilute Grey (Silver) or the Dominant Dilute Fawn (Cream) as it would seem that the first birds may have been poorly coloured cream suffused Silvers. In the 1940's Dominant Silvers were then being bred in Europe from, it was said, imported Australian stock.

The Dominant Dilute character can be carried in either single or double quantities and in both cases the visual expression is the same. By adding the Dominant Dilute character to a Normal Grey Zebra Finch the Dominant Silver as it is mostly called is evolved. If a Normal Grey cock or hen is paired to a Silver having a single quantity of the Dominant Dilute character they will produce 50% Silver having single quantity of

Dominant Dilute and 50% pure Normal Greys. Any Normal Greys bred from such pairings will be equally as pure genetically as if both parents had been pure Normal Greys. Should the Dominant Silver used have been carrying a double quantity of the Dominant Dilute character all the young would have been Dominant Silvers with a single quantity. In the first instance double quantity birds can be bred by the pairing together of two single quantity Dominant Silvers. The theoretical expectation of such crosses is 25% pure Normal Grey, 50% Dominant Silver single quantity and 25% Dominant Silver double quantity.

At one time considerable quantities of really good coloured Dominant Silvers were to be seen in the aviaries of breeders and at shows up and down the country. During the last few years Dominant Silvers have rather fallen from favour and have been replaced by the Dominant Creams. This is mainly due I think to the fact that in the process of breeding the Dominant Cream birds Dominant Silvers were used to outcross with Fawns. After a generation or two the Dominant Silvers that were evolved from these cross pairings showed heavy pale fawnish tinting on their backs and wings making them two tone birds. Breeders found some difficulty in eliminating this suffusion from the Silvers and in many cases went over to the breeding of Creams.

I feel certain that the success in breeding good solid coloured Dominant Silvers is by using only level coloured Normal Greys as outcrosses and this is supported by my own breeding results. If Dominant Silvers are selected for their nearness to the ideal colour and are mated to sound level coloured Normal Greys the end result after a few generations will be Dominant Silvers of the real silver grey shade. The actual depth of the silver shade will be controlled by the depth of colour of the Normal Greys used in their production. Careful selection of the birds must be made with each pairing if the ultimate goal is to be achieved in the shortest possible time. Every effort should be made not to use Fawns, "split" Fawns, Creams, or any colours that have been bred through Fawns or Fawn carrying stock. If this principle is strictly observed the breeder will have Dominant Silvers that are really a level silver grey shade of colour.

Colour description
COCK. Eyes dark (shades of dark red or brown). Beak bright red. Feet and legs pinkish. Head silvery grey with some dark ticking to centre of head. Neck, back and wings silvery grey. Chest bar sooty to light grey. Throat to upper breast bar grey zebra lines on a white ground running from cheek to cheek. Tear marks grey. Cheek lobes can vary from pale cream to pale orange. Underparts below bar white. Tail grey with white barrings, side flankings reddish to pinkish fawn ornamented with many small white spots.
HEN. As other hens but of the same shade of dilution to match cocks. Beak paler red.
Show colour faults: Light edges to wing feathers, fawn or cream tinting on back and upper wings, irregular chest bar, too narrow or poorly spotted side flankings and blotchy overall colouring. Indistinct tear marks. Traces of chest barring on hens.

Recessive Silver Zebra Finches
From what I have been able to discover the first Recessive Dilutes were bred in Denmark during approximately the same period as the Dominant Dilutes appeared in Australia. It is fairly certain that

these birds were the Recessive Dilute form of the Normal Greys and that it was some years later before the Recessive Dilute Fawns—the Creams—were produced from them. Like their Dominant counterparts they too can be bred in different depths of colouring corresponding to the shade of the Normal Greys from which they are derived. The general run of Recessive Silvers are deeper in colour than the Dominant kind and are usually much more even in their overall colouring. The deep shaded Recessive Silvers are frequently called "Blues" in Europe but they are not a separate mutation contrary to what was thought at one time. I have paired these Continental "Blues" to British bred Recessive Silvers and all the young they have produced have been shades of silver showing that both birds belong to one and the same Recessive mutation.

The breeding of Recessive Silvers is quite different to that of the Dominant kind and it naturally takes longer to produce and improve this mutation. When a Recessive Silver either cock or hen is mated to a Normal Grey all the resulting young are normal grey in colour but carry the Recessive Dilute character in their genetical makeup. By pairing two of these Normal "split" Recessive Silvers together the theoretical expectation is 25% pure Normal Greys, 50% Normal Grey/Recessive Silvers and 25% pure Recessive Silvers. Once again there is no visual way of distinguishing between the two genetical kinds of Normal Greys that are produced except by test pairings to Recessive Silvers. The pairing together of two Recessive Silvers will give only Recessive Silver young.

It will be observed by the above theoretical expectations that the Recessive Dilute character reproduces in just the same way as do all other Recessive characters.

This being so it therefore takes longer to establish a Recessive strain than it does a Dominant one. Undoubtedly this fact has done much to cause the Dominant kind to become far more popular than the more difficult Recessive type. The colour of most of the Recessive Silvers is deeper and more inclined to be level than in the Dominant even if it is not quite so distinctive. The so-called "Blue" Zebra Finches have I think been evolved by the selective pairings of the brightest coloured Recessive Silvers and they make most attractively coloured birds. Many of the hens in the Recessive Silver series show ghost ear lobes which certainly adds to their appearance.

I have found the best way to maintain good colour and to improve Recessive Silvers overall is to mate them only to first cross Normal Grey "split" for Recessive Silver. By first cross "splits" I mean to indicate birds that have been bred from selected pure Normal Greys matched with selected Recessive Silvers. To achieve continuity of this method a number of first cross "splits" will have to be bred each year otherwise progress will not be sustained. Very few Recessive Dilutes have been seen on the Show benches during the past decade although quite presentable specimens do exist in some breeders' aviaries. If good specimens could be seen I feel sure they would attract more breeders.

Colour description

COCK. Eyes dark (shades of dark red or brown). Beak red. Feet and legs pinkish. Head silvery medium grey with some dark ticking to centre of head. Neck, back and wings, silvery grey to bluish grey. Chest bar sooty to grey. Throat to upper chest bar grey zebra lines on a white ground from cheek to cheek. Tear marks grey.

Cheek lobes can vary from reddish orange to pale orange. Underparts below bar white. Tail grey with white barrings, side flankings shades of reddish fawn ornamented with small white spots.

HEN. As other hens but of the same shade of dilution to match cocks. Beak paler red.

Show colour faults: Light edges to wing feathers, fawn tinting on back and upper wings, irregular chest bar, too narrow or poorly spotted side flankings and blotchy overall colouring. Indistinct tear marks. Traces of chest barring on hens.

Chapter 8

CREAM ZEBRA FINCHES

Dominant Cream Zebra Finches

As I explained in the previous Chapter it is difficult to know for certain just when the Dominant Dilute character appeared as a mutation beyond the fact it happened in Australia. This matters little now as we have many fine strains of these delicately coloured Zebra Finches that have become so popular both as exhibition and aviary stock. Their popularity is really quite understandable as the colour of Dominant Creams is delicate, soft, and pleasing to the eye, and much more inclined to evenness of colour than are their Silver counterparts.

Being the Dominant Dilute form of the Fawn, two sets of characters are involved in their production—the Dominant of the Dilute and the Sex-linked of the Fawn. Dominant Creams are fortunately reasonably plentiful nowadays so breeders need not start from scratch as it were by using the Dominant Silver × Fawn matings to produce the desired colour. When a Fawn of either sex is paired to a single character Dominant Cream the resulting young are Fawn cocks and hens and Dominant Cream cocks and hens, quite a nice straightforward result. The colouring of Creams from such crosses will depend to a great extent on the actual shade of the Fawns used.

Care should be exercised when selecting the Fawns to ensure they are of a good rich medium shade so that the resulting creams will be clearly marked and their colour soft but yet distinctive. If the very dark kind of Fawns are used the Creams produced may well be too strong in colour and difficult to distinguish from extra light Fawns. Likewise very light Fawns should be avoided as the Creams they produce will be far too pale in colour and markings. Each breeding pair should be mated for their good colouring properties and at the same time should be substantially built and of the correct type.

Should the breeder wish to establish a strain of Dominant Creams from Dominant Silvers and Fawns the following theoretical expectations will serve as a guide. The sex of the Fawns used in these matings will have a definite influence on the colour of the young they produce. Fawn cocks to single character Silver hens will give 25% Normal Grey/Fawn cocks, 25% single character Silver/Cream (Fawn) cocks, 25% Fawn hens and 25% single character Cream hens. If the mating is reversed and single character Silver cocks are paired to Fawn hens they will give 25% Normal Grey/Fawn cocks, 25% single character Silver/Cream (Fawn) cocks, 25% Normal Grey hens and 25% single character Silver hens. Both of these matings indicate how the Dominant Dilute character works quite independently of the other characters. The first mating is obviously the best as it gives the breeder a number of single character Cream hens. The next step is to mate these single character Cream hens to Fawn cocks and then both Cream and Fawn in cocks and hens will result.

Although Dominant Creams seem to show less patchiness of colour than do the Dominant Silvers it is nevertheless extremely important to only use for breeding birds that are as near as possible to the ideal colour. It appears that after a few seasons of careful selecting of the breeding stock the number of good coloured birds rises sharply. Even when this peak is reached it is still necessary to maintain a strict watch on the colour of all the birds used. A few careless pairings can quickly set the stud back several years and this is something that should not be allowed to happen.

Colour description

COCK. Eyes dark (shades of dark red or brown). Beak bright red. Feet and legs pink. Head cream with some darker tickings to centre of head. Neck, back and wings, pale cream to deep cream. Chest bar, sooty brown to brownish grey. Throat to upper chest bar, paler shades of sooty brown to brownish grey zebra lines on a white ground running from cheek to cheek. Tear marks greyish. Underparts below bar, white. Tail light greyish with white barrings, side flankings shades of reddish fawn ornamented with small white spots.

HEN. As other hens but of the same shade of dilution to match cocks. Beak paler red.

Show colour faults: Light edges to wing feathers, irregular chest bar, too narrow or poorly spotted side flankings, blotchy overall colouring and not enough contrast between body colour and markings. Indistinct tear marks. Traces of chest barring on hens.

Recessive Cream Zebra Finches

It would seem that several different forms of Recessive Creams have made their appearance although the majority of examples seen at the present time have been produced from crossing Recessive Silvers with Fawns. This combination will give birds which have the colouring of the Recessive Dilutes in the Cream form. By mating a Fawn cock to a Recessive Silver hen the theoretical expectation is all Normal Grey "split" for Fawn and Recessive Dilute cocks and all Fawn "split" for Recessive Dilute hens. The next pairing of Normal Grey/Fawn Recessive Dilute cock to Fawn/Recessive Dilute hen gives Fawn cocks and hens, Normal Grey cocks and hens and Recessive Dilute (Cream) cocks and hens.

Several breeders, including myself, have had birds belonging to a different Recessive Dilute mutation for Cream where the Fawn character was not involved. My first experience with this mutation was when I bred a Recessive Cream cock from a pair of Normal Greys. The parentage of this pair of Normal Greys was not known but the Recessive Cream cock was the only "odd" colour produced by them out of a dozen or so youngsters. This Recessive Cream cock was paired to two different unrelated Normal Grey hens and they produced only normal grey coloured young both cocks and hens. Several pairs of these half brothers and sisters were mated and they in turn gave a number of Recessive Cream cocks and hens. A rather unusual feature of this mutation was that only Creams were bred—no Silvers appearing from any of the many pairings. I have also had reports of similar results from other British and Continental breeders. Owing to shortage of aviary space I had to dispose of all my stock of these Recessive Dilutes to make room for other experimental pairs. At the moment I do not know how this particular strain has progressed.

For show purposes both Dominant and Recessive Creams need to be most carefully matched for shade and evenness of colour. It will be found that there can be considerable variation in depth of shade even with young birds bred from the same parent. I have seen pairs very good for substance, matching size and level

2. *A Cream cock and a Silver hen.*

3. *A Silver pair and a Cream cock.*

4. *A Fawn Pied cock and a pair of Normal Grey Pieds.*

5. *A Penguin cock, a Fawn cock and a Normal Grey hen.*

colour fail because of the contrast between their actual depth of shade. Well matched pairs of Creams of any depth make really attractive show birds.

Colour description

COCK. Eyes dark (shades of dark red or brown). Beak bright red. Feet and legs pink. Head cream with some darker ticking to centre of head. Neck, back and wings, shades of deep cream to pale fawn. Chest bar sooty to dark grey. Throat to upper chest bar paler shades of sooty to dark grey zebra lines on a white ground running from cheek to cheek. Tear marks dark greyish. Underparts below bar white. Tail dark greyish with white barrings, side flankings shades of bright reddish fawn ornamented with small white dots.
HEN. As other hens but with the same shade of dilution to match cocks. Beak paler red.

Show colour faults: Light edges to wing feathers, irregular chest bar, too narrow or poorly spotted side flankings. Blotchy overall colouring and not enough contrast between body colour and markings. Indistinct tear marks. Traces of chest barring on hens.

Fawn Pied Zebra Finches (cock on the right).

Chapter 9

PIED ZEBRA FINCHES

When a species becomes thoroughly domesticated new colour mutations invariably occur and in addition to these other mutations appear that have the effect of causing the plumage colouring to become broken with areas devoid of pigment. Such specimens are known in the Cage Bird Fancy as variegated or pied birds and in the Zebra Finch we have the Recessive Pied which can be bred in all colour forms. The Pied Zebra Finches were not the first of the colour mutations and examples were not recorded until about 1935/6. Before this odd birds had been bred with white ticks or a few white flight feathers but these did not reproduce their mismarkings. The only Pied mutation so far noted appeared in a mixed aviary collection in Denmark and it was from these birds that all the present day Pied Zebra Finches have descended. This Pied mutation is Recessive in its mode of inheritance and there can be very big differences in the amount of the clear areas shown by individual specimens. It is quite within the bounds of possibility that further Pied mutations will occur like in the Budgerigars where there are both Dominant and Recessive Pied kinds.

From an exhibition angle the best looking birds are the Pied forms of the Normal Grey and the Fawn as these give the most distinctive patterns. For the interested colour breeders other colour mutations in Pieds are most fascinating to produce even if the end products are not always very striking in their colouring.

There are of course various ways in which Pied Zebra Finches can be produced and I think the following pairings give the most satisfactory results as to their colour and markings.

Because a Recessive mutation is being dealt with the Pied partner in an initial pairing can be of either sex and Normal Grey paired to Pied Normal Grey gives all Normal Grey/Pied young. However the Normal Grey partner should be a good example of its colour and the Pied mate should be as near to the standard colour pattern as possible. If birds with too much white or dark areas are used there is always a strong tendency for these forms to be reproduced when Pieds reappear in the second generation. Pied to Normal Grey/Pied gives 50 % of each kind and Normal Grey/Pied to Normal Grey/Pied produces 25 % Pieds, 50 % Normal Grey/Pieds and 25 % pure Normal Greys. Whenever possible only first cross "splits" should be used and it is therefore necessary to breed a number of such birds each season when maintaining a stud of Pieds.

When it comes to the breeding of Pied Fawns the sex of the Fawns used does help to produce the desired colour more quickly. Fawn cock to Normal Grey Pied hen gives Normal Grey/Fawn Pied cocks and Fawn/Pied hens. Such birds paired together gives 25 % Pied cocks and hens and some will be Pied Fawns. Once having produced Pied Fawns their numbers can rapidly be increased by crossing Pied Fawn cocks with Fawn/Pied hens where all the Pieds bred will be of the Fawn kind. I know that many breeders consider Pied Fawns to be the most handsome of all the Pied varieties and well matched pairs are certainly most attractive.

For exhibition, Pieds have to be most carefully chosen to ensure that both members of the pairs show similar areas of the correct variegation. The matching of pairs is of utmost importance with show birds and it is one that is inclined to be neglected sometimes in favour of size. The broken cock pattern markings are essential in all good well balanced exhibition pairs and this applies equally to ear lobes, side flankings, chest bar and zebra markings. When selecting pairs for show the colour descriptions at the end of each chapter should be carefully studied.

Colour description

COCK. Eyes dark (shades of dark red or brown). Beak coral red. Feet and legs red to pink. Normal Grey (or its mutant colours) broken with approximately 50 % of white (white underparts not to be included in the 50 %). All markings on cheeks, chest and flanks to be retained in broken form. Tear and tail markings distinct but can be broken.

HEN. As other hens to match cocks for pied markings and depth of colour. Beaks paler red.

Show colour faults: Loss of cock markings, unbroken cock markings, too large or too small areas of white. Traces of chest barring on hens.

Pair of Penguin Zebra Finches having settled down for the night on their clutch of eggs.

Chapter 10

PENGUIN ZEBRA FINCHES

The Zebra Finches now universally known as Penguins
are yet another mutation which has its origin in
Australia. Their history is somewhat obscure but they
were being aviary bred in their native home in the
1940s. Penguins were first produced in Europe by L.
Raymaekers of Brussels, Belgium, sometime about
1949/50 and examples reached Great Britain two or
three years later. At first they were known as White-
Bellied or Silverwings and both of these names are
quite descriptive of the mutation up to a point. As the
underparts of other Zebra Finch mutations are white
and Silvers actually have silver coloured wings the
name Penguin was coined and soon found favour
everywhere.

This mutation is again Recessive and produces a
dilution of colour together with the loss of throat zebra
markings and chest bar. The absence of markings on
the chest gives a complete sweep of white from chin to
vent, hence the appropriate name Penguin. Although
there can be Penguin forms of other mutations it is
only the Normal Grey and Fawn kinds that give a really
satisfactory colour result. Penguin forms of Silvers,
Creams, Chestnut-flanked Whites, or Pieds, lack contrast by being too pallid thereby reducing the attrac-
tion. After their second moult Penguins develop a
lacing effect on back and upper wings adding further
to their appeal both as aviary and exhibition birds.
Having a dilute colouring, Penguins will be found to

vary a little in their actual depth of overall colouring and this is often noticeable between individual strains.

The original Penguins imported from Europe were smaller, longer, tighter feathered birds, than the varieties already well established and it has taken a considerable time to eradicate these characters from the Penguins. Their progress has I think been hampered somewhat by this failing of type and the resulting reluctance of breeders to take up this mutation. Fortunately a few dedicated enthusiasts have persevered and their efforts have resulted in much improved strains of both Normal Grey and Fawn Penguins.

A Penguin Normal Grey paired to a pure Normal Grey gives 100% Normal Grey/Penguin young and these when mated back to further Penguin Normal Greys will produce 50% Penguin Normal Greys and 50% Normal Grey/Penguins. Here again only first cross "splits" should be used if improvement of type and substance is to take place and be maintained. Frequently the best quality Penguin Normal Greys have been bred from the mating together of two first cross "splits". The result of such crosses is 25% Penguin Normal Greys, 50% Normal Grey/Penguins and 25% pure Normal Greys and is often considered to be wasteful as 75% of the young are normal grey coloured birds of unknown genetical makeup. The overall quality of the Penguins so produced is usually excellent and they make first rate partners for the breeding of further first cross "splits".

Sex-linkage again plays an important part in the initial breeding of Penguin Fawns and I would suggest that the first matings should be Fawn cocks to Penguin Normal Grey hens. The theoretical expectations from this cross are 50% Normal Grey/Penguin Fawn cocks and 50% Fawn/Penguin hens. When these two genetical kinds are paired together they give 25 % Penguin young half of which will be Penguin Fawn cocks and hens. In the following season Penguin Fawn cocks can be mated to Fawn/Penguin hens and all the young produced will be of fawn colouring.

I have seen both Penguin Silvers and Penguin Creams but in my opinion their colouring is far too pale and nondescript and the attractiveness of both kinds is lost. From a colour breeding angle it is of great interest to produce composite varieties and the Penguin character can be used to produce complex types.

With the breeding of Penguins in all colours care must be taken when mating up the breeding pairs to ensure that type and substance are always present. If this is not done the general standard of the stock will remain static.

Colour description

Penguin Normal Grey
COCK. Eyes dark (shades of dark red or brown). Beak bright red. Feet and legs pinkish. Head, neck and wings light, even silver grey, with flights, secondaries and coverts edged with a paler shade of grey giving a laced effect. (This lacing does not show to full advantage until after the second and subsequent full moults). Underparts from cheek to vent pure white without any trace of markings or barring. Cheek lobes pale cream to pale orange to match shade of body colour. Tail silvery grey barred with white. Side flankings reddish brown ornamented with clear white spots.
HEN. As other hens but with cheek lobes white. Beak paler red.

Show colour faults: Barring on chest of cocks and traces of barring on hens. Lack of lacing on wings.

Penguin Fawn

As for Penguin Normal Grey except that all the silver grey areas are replaced by a pale fawn colouring.

Show colour faults: These are the same as for Penguin Normal Grey.

Penguin Zebra Finch cock showing only a faint trace of the chest bar—a show fault.

Chapter 11

YELLOW-BEAKED ZEBRA FINCHES

For many years the Yellow-beaked mutation passed unrecorded by breeders; it is therefore very difficult to estimate when these birds first arrived and from where. In the wild in Australia there are two races of Long-tailed Grassfinches—the Common Longtailed Grass-finches which have yellow coloured beaks and the Heck's Longtailed Grassfinches where the beaks are red. Both of these kinds which are coloured alike are to be found breeding in the wild and at times their territories overlap and cross pairing is said to occur. It is quite possible that Yellow-beaked Zebra Finches were also produced in wild flocks of Normal Greys and have passed unnoticed. With the exception of their beak colour they are almost like the normal beaked kind and could have been imported during the times when Zebra Finches were coming freely from Australia. The Yellow-beaked character is Recessive and an odd bird here and there could be crossed in with Normal pairs and would give only normal beaked young. Yellow-beaks would not reappear again until two birds "split" for the character happened by chance to be mated together. Until such a cross was made the Recessive character would be handed down from generation to generation quite unbeknown to the breeder.

The first Yellow-beaked birds I actually handled were during the middle of the 1950s and these were bred in aviaries in two places in the Midlands of England. Since then I have examined numbers of Yellow-beaked

Greys, Yellow-beaked Fawns and Yellow-beaked Whites and with the exception of the last named their colour was just very slightly paler and less bright in tone when compared alongside their normal beaked counterparts. The colour difference is so small that it can be overlooked unless the specimens are examined very closely. Most of the birds I have seen were bred by chance and their yellow beaks varied quite a lot in brightness, shade and depth of colour. A few purposely bred examples showed a definite improvement in their richness of beak shade. With some selective pairings over a few seasons I feel sure that Yellow-beaked birds could be produced showing a really outstanding beak colour. Such birds would be a welcome addition to the classes as they are likely to be birds of good type and substance.

I make the following suggestions for breeding Yellow-beaked Zebra Finches for those breeders who actually have examples in their aviaries. As Yellow-beaks paired to any of the other normal beaked varieties give only normal beaked young they should first be paired to normal beaked birds of their own colour; for example, Yellow-beaked Normal Grey to Normal Grey, Yellow-beaked White to White, Yellow-beaked Fawn to Fawn etc. By using top quality normal beaked birds for outcrossing and paying particular attention to see that they have soundly coloured beaks the ultimate Yellow-beaks bred will have fine rich deep orange yellow coloured beaks. The "split" birds from such matings will when paired to Yellow-beaked mates give 50% Normal/Yellow-beaked and 50% Yellow-beaked cocks and hens. At present the most usual pairings because of the shortage of stock are "split" Yellow-beaked to "split" Yellow-beaked which gives 25% Yellow-beaked young. Two Yellow-beaked paired together will give 100% Yellow-beaked young no matter what is the colour of the adult birds. For instance, a Yellow-beaked Fawn cock paired to a Yellow-beaked White hen will give all Yellow-beaked Normal Grey/Fawn White cock and all Yellow-beaked Fawn/White hens.

Colour description

Yellow-beaked Normal Grey

COCK. Eyes dark (shades of dark red or brown). Beak shades of rich yellow to orange yellow. Feet and legs pink, red or reddish brown. Head dull dark grey with some darker tickings to centre of head. Neck, back and wings dull grey. Chest bar black. Throat and upper breast above bar black, zebra lines on a white ground running from cheek to cheek. Tear marks black. Cheek lobes reddish orange, Underparts below bar white with some slight fawnish tinting in vent area. Tail black with white barrings, side flankings reddish brown ornamented with many small white spots.
HEN. As other hens to match cock. Beak paler yellow shades.

Show colour faults: Light edgings to wing feathers, irregular chest bar, too narrow or poorly spotted flankings and blotchy overall colouring. Indistinct tear markings. Traces of chest barring on hens.

There can be Yellow-beaked forms of all other colours and these can be estimated by looking at the other colour descriptions and substituting the yellow beak.

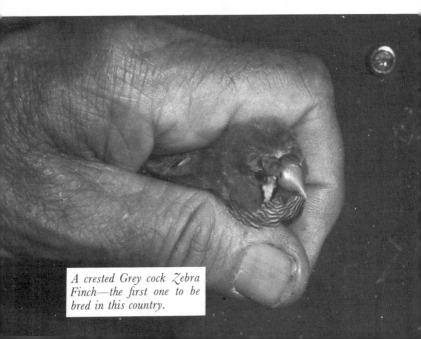

A crested Grey cock Zebra
Finch—the first one to be
bred in this country.

Chapter 12

CRESTED ZEBRA FINCHES

Most mutations amongst cage and aviary birds affect the colouring of their plumage but there is one that occurs in domesticated species that alters the feather formation in special areas, particularly the head, causing crests to be formed. Such species as Canaries, Budgerigars, Bengalese and certain Pigeons have had Crested forms for a very long time and the appearance of crests amongst Zebra Finches was therefore not unexpected. The first Crested Zebra Finches were reported by that noted bird artist and ornithologist Herman Heinzel who in the late 1960s observed two Normal Greys in Spain that had small crests on their heads. Since that time several other Crested Zebra Finches have been bred in a number of European countries and strains of them are now being evolved. Although Crested birds are not popular with all breeders there is always a nucleus who like to develop unusual or different mutations. This being so I feel sure that Crested Zebra Finches in all colour mutations will in due course be established and produced in exhibition type birds. Their appearance has certainly added a further dimension to the fast growing cult of Zebra Finch breeding and exhibiting.

The feather mutation that causes the head crest is a Dominant one and the actual shape of the crest seems to be governed to some extent by modifying agents in the birds' genetical makeup. With Crested Canaries there is an associated lethal factor when two Crested birds are paired together producing a percentage of young having two characters for the Crested character. It would appear that such birds die either in the egg or soon after hatching. This lethal action does not seem to apply to Pigeons and possibly Budgerigars but the position of the Bengalese has not yet been fully investigated. This fact being a possibility it is therefore logical to follow the Canary method of breeding when dealing with the production of Crested Zebra Finches.

When a Crested bird is paired to a non Crested example the resulting young are either crested or non crested and the latter are called Crestbred. These Crestbreds appear to have a greater potential to produce actual Crested birds when paired to Crests than do "pure" non Crested birds. The usual mating procedure in breeding and developing Crested types is to

A pair of Cream Zebra Finches.

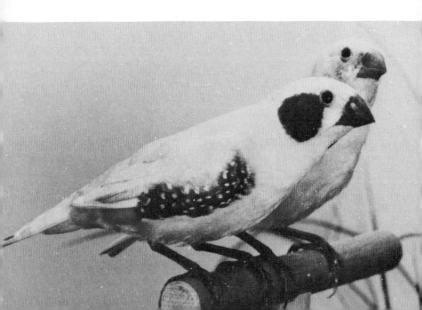

6. *A Penguin pair.*

mate Crested to Crestbred and the theoretical expectation is 50% of each kind.

Being in their very early stages of development Crested Zebra Finches will need to be selectively bred to improve the shape and size of the crest itself. From information received it would appear that the Crested birds vary in the quality of the crests they carry. Some have feathers of different lengths very roughly in a circular formation, others have feathers sticking up forming a tuft, and a few have a neat flat circular crest. These different types of crests have all been bred from the same stock so it would appear that strict control of their breeding is required to get continuity in the reproduction of good flat circular crests. They are like the Yellow-beaked mutation in the respect that their colour has no effect whatsoever on the production of the crest. There can be Crested birds in all colours and as the Crest character is Dominant it can quickly be passed from one colour to another. At this juncture of their production I would suggest that every cross made should be Crest to Crestbred except when the crest is desired to be transferred on to another colour form.

As far as I am aware Crested Zebra Finches have not yet been seen anywhere on the show benches but they should be in the not too distant future. It is the accepted practice with other Crested varieties of birds to show pairs consisting of one Crest and one Crestbred. The Crestbred partners for show purposes could well be "pure" non Crested as there is no visual difference between these non Crested kind. Again it would be immaterial whether the cock or the hen of a pair carries the crest providing both birds belong to the same colour mutation. To date I have produced the following colour mutations all with nice flat round crests: White; Chestnut-flanked White; Light back; and Black-breasted in addition to Normal Grey.

Colour description

COCK OR HEN. These are coloured exactly the same as described for the Normal Grey and all its colour mutations, the only difference being they should have a small flat circular crest situated centrally on the head and the feathers should radiate evenly from a centre point.

Crestbred
COCK OR HEN. These are coloured exactly the same as described for the Normal Grey and all its colour mutations.

Show colour faults: As for all other Zebra Finches.

Chapter 13

COLOUR MUTATIONS
NOT YET ESTABLISHED

In addition to the mutations already described in the previous Chapters there are several others that are in the process of being developed. Information about the various aspects of these birds is not always complete and the descriptions of the same birds can vary somewhat between countries and from breeder to breeder.

Black Zebra Finches

For a long time now Black and partially Black Zebra Finch cocks and hens have been turning up in breeding establishments in various parts of the world. I have seen a few cock birds that in their nest and first adult plumage have been almost completely black except for dark red brown ear lobes and side flanks, the latter being devoid of the characteristic white spots. Hen birds from the same nests have again been mainly black except for dark greyish underparts. These Black specimens have either died before being used for breeding or have moulted out more or less like dark Normal Greys. Where such birds have reproduced their young have unfortunately all been quite normal in their colouring. Birds with patches of black mainly on face, neck and chest areas have again moulted out into ordinary looking birds. One unusual thing about these Blacks is that nearly all of them have been bred from birds having the Fawn character in their makeup. From this it can be deduced that this excess of black pigment is due to a pigment breakdown and is not genetical and hereditary. Nevertheless it is prudent that all such birds should if possible be experimented with as there must always be the possibility of a black mutation occurring.

Black-breasted Zebra Finches

It would appear that there are at least two separate mutations that give birds having solid black on the upper half of the breast from the chin. One mutation is breeding in Australian aviaries and the other in European establishments and both seem to have many features in common. I will discuss the Australian kind first; these are called Black-faced or Black-fronted by their breeders. Such birds have solid black upper breasts and some also have black on the vent area. I am not sure how they are coloured otherwise except they may be a little darker in overall colouring than the usual Normal Greys. The inheritance of this Black-fronted kind has not yet been completely unravelled. It seems that there is a possibility that it is a Dominant as in some pairings of Black-fronted cocks to Normal Grey hens both Black-fronted and Normal Grey young have resulted. Some breeders have mated hens bred from one Black-fronted parent to Black-fronted cocks and again have bred Black-fronted and Normal Greys. The actual number of young so far bred from Black-fronted stock is limited; therefore it is a little early to draw definite conclusions although it certainly looks as though the character may be a Dominant one.

I have a fuller picture of the colouring of the European mutation which in Germany is called Schwarzbrust (Black-breast). The cocks have orange brown cheek lobes that are more extensive than those on other colours, without the usual tear marks, white chin with some black spots followed by solid black half way down the breast then pure white to vent. The side flankings are orange brown ornamented with small white bars and not spots. The rump is white with the tail pale beige without barring but some feathers have black centre shafts and the tail is tipped with black. The head, neck, back and wings are medium dark grey with some brownish edging to wing feathers. The hens have pale grey cheek lobes with white chin and grey upper breast followed by pale beige to the vent. The head, neck, back, wings and tail, are coloured like those of the cocks. Here again the inheritance of this character is not yet fully understood but it is thought to be Recessive. It would appear that both the Australian and European mutations could be one and the same. These birds certainly have an intriguing colour pattern and should make useful birds for further colour breeding and of course exhibiting.

Grizzle Zebra Finches

During the late 1960s yet another Zebra Finch mutation appeared in Australia where they have been descriptively named Grizzle Zebra Finches. This particular pattern mutation has been established and already produced in several different colour forms. These Grizzles can be had in all colours except of course Albinos, Whites and Chestnut-flanked Whites and have already been bred in most colours by their enthusiastic breeders. The difference between this mutation and the other kinds is that their whole body including ear lobes and flankings are covered with tiny white dots giving a pepper and salt or frosted effect. A few examples have arrived in Great Britain and breeding experiments are now under way in an effort to discover their breeding behaviour. At one time it was thought they were Dominant but experimental results so far do not seem to completely support this assumption. It could well be that the spotting does not appear until after the birds get their full adult plumage similar to the lacing on the Penguins. It can be imagined that birds with this colouring are most attractive but it will be a considerable time before they are readily obtainable in this country.

Light Back Zebra Finches

For a number of years reports have come from Europe of the existence of a mutation which seems to be a variation of the Normal Grey. I believe that these birds were first noticed and investigated under the name of Hellrucken by Professor Dr. H. Steiner of Zurich. From my discussions with overseas visitors it appears that the Light Back variety is now reasonably well known in European countries. Up to the present time I have not seen or heard about any specimens being in this country. From colour transparencies and colour prints I have seen Light Backs are a slightly dilute form of the Normal Grey with the exception of the black and white areas. The cheek lobes and side flankings are more orange and less in depth than Normal Greys with the head, neck, back and wings a clear pale brown grey shade.

The inheritance of this mutation does not seem to be quite clear although there is a distinct possibility of it being Recessive. It is always a little difficult to sort out facts without knowing full details of pedigrees and breeding results and of course not seeing the birds themselves. A further point that does not yet seem clear is whether there can be other colour forms of the Light Back. It has occurred to me that this mutation could in fact be the reappearance of one of the original sub species from Australia which went into the melting pot in the early days of the domestication of the Zebra Finch. No doubt in course of time all these points will be clarified.

Further details on the Light-Backs

Two seasons ago Herman Heinzel kindly sent me a Light-back cock which I mated to a Chestnut-flanked White hen as suggested by Continental breeders. Out of nine young from the pair there were three Light-back cocks and six Chestnut-flanked White cocks and hens. This season having only cock Light-backs I again used Chestnut-flanked White hens as mates and so far have bred some fifteen Light-backs and about twenty Chestnut-flanked Whites, both cocks and hens. From this it would seem that the Light-back original cock was "split" for Chestnut-flanked White and that the Light-back character is Dominant to the Chestnut-flanked White. Now having produced Light-back hens which will not be "split" for the Sex-linked Chestnut-flanked White character I can try crossing them with pure Normals and together to try and discover their exact manner of inheritance.

Saddle Back Zebra Finches

From time to time White Zebra Finches have been bred with a distinct grey or fawn saddle or mantle patch. I have seen a number of such birds and as the cocks do not show the characteristic cock markings I have come to the conclusion they must be a form of White. By selective breeding with ordinary Whites that show a lot of back flecking it is very possible that Saddle backs could arise. On the other hand they could be a further mutation from the White. Until controlled experimental tests have been made it will not be possible to say just what these birds may be. I must say here that both cocks and hens do have this particular saddle patch. Evenly marked pairs would make quite good exhibition birds whatever their hereditary peculiarities may be.

Further Zebra Finch colours

A new White kind is being developed in America that is coloured like the Chestnut-flanked White but the cocks are without any marking on back or chest.

It is fairly certain that with the extensive breeding of Zebra Finches all over the world even more colour mutations will be occurring in the future. I would certainly urge any breeder who finds unusual coloured Zebra Finches amongst the breeding flocks to report particulars to a Zebra Finch Society or an experienced breeder. If this is done any possible new mutation can be investigated and developed and something different may be discovered. Should a mutation be discovered and it happens to be a hen the colour change may only be slight and could pass unnoticed if a careful watch is not maintained.

A further possibility of colour and pattern changes is of course through the use of fertile Hybrids. It is well known that Zebra Finches will cross quite freely with numerous other small Foreign birds. From such crosses it may be possible that some of the cock Hybrids will be fertile and when back crossed to Zebra Finches produce further birds which will in turn introduce new patterns or colours into the Zebra Finch.

Chapter 14

HOUSING

Undoubtedly one of the big factors that has contributed to the ever growing popularity of Zebra Finches is their ability to live and thrive in a great variety of housing conditions. This means that they can be kept and bred both in cages and aviaries of less size than many other species of cage and aviary birds. Nevertheless they should not be subjected to cramped or overcrowded conditions if they are to be successful in all respects. Zebra Finches will live and breed in cages, indoor flights (pens) and outdoor aviaries of designs to suit their owner's particular requirements.

In many urban areas there are size restrictions on garden buildings and the usual permitted garden shed can easily be converted into most suitable accommodation for Zebra Finches. Such buildings have space for a series of tiered cages and one or two small indoor flights. Cages should be as near as possible to 1m (3ft) long, 45cm (18in) high and 38cm (15in) deep. The actual measurements can be adjusted so that the tiers are accommodated in the available space of the building. Punch bar cage fronts of various sizes with a large central door can be obtained at most bird stores. The large door is really necessary for easy cleaning, moving nest boxes and ringing young birds. The cages themselves can be made from plywood, wooden boarding, manufactured board sheets and a mixture of these materials, and decorated internally with white emulsion paint and externally with the same or another paint not containing lead. Such cages are suitable for holding one breeding pair or eight to ten non breeding birds. In every kind of accommodation overcrowding must be avoided to prevent undue squabbling and to give the birds themselves sufficient freedom for easy movement.

If the cages are made in tiered rows of say three cages wide by four deep, each separated by a movable wooden partition, they can be quickly converted into most useful flights when not being used for breeding. This is a big advantage blocks of cages have over single cage units. Most owners fit sand drawers to their cages but these are not absolutely essential although they are most useful when cleaning.

Seed, water and grit are best given in small flat vessels made of glass, metal, plastic or earthenware. These should not be placed directly under perches or nest boxes but on a small table or ledge to prevent the contents from being fouled. The perches themselves should be of varying thicknesses to allow foot exercise for the birds and can be made from all kinds of wood with or without bark. Perches should be renewed periodically and this is no problem as there is such a variety of wood from which to choose. I have mentioned in several of my books that the dried stems of herbaceous garden plants of the Golden Rod and Michaelmas Daisy families make excellent perches for Zebra Finches. It is best I find to cut the stems soon after the flowers have dried, the leaves should then be stripped, and the stems allowed to thoroughly dry. They will keep in good condition for a very long time when stored in a dry airy place. Good well fixed perches make for the maximum fertility amongst the stock of any cage and aviary birds.

Although breeding results from cage breeding pairs are relatively good those obtained from the use of flights and aviaries are invariably better. The flight (or pen) method takes up more space and would often mean the curtailing of the number of pairs put up for breeding. This is mostly counter-balanced by the greater number of young produced in the larger structures. Like cages, flights can be made in various sizes to fit in the space available and a good size is 2m ($6\frac{1}{2}$ft) high, 1.5m ($4\frac{1}{2}$ft) deep and .5m ($1\frac{1}{2}$ft) wide. Each flight will accommodate two breeding pairs or up to twenty non breeding birds. These flights can be made of small mesh wire netting on light wooden battens which can be decorated with non lead containing paint or emulsion paint. The entrance doors should be made as low as possible so as to prevent escapes whilst entering the flights. Perching and seed, water and grit vessels are the same as for cages. Flight and cage floors can be covered with fine gravel, coarse sawdust, washed sand or a mixture of these materials. Sand and gravel will provide the birds with an extra source of grits and mineral elements.

From a decorative point of view outdoor flighted aviaries are the best for keeping and breeding Zebra Finches. With this kind of accommodation the owner has little control over the breeding pairs which is so very necessary when producing exhibition birds or for colour breeding. Nevertheless thousands of Zebra Finch enthusiasts all over the world get great pleasure from their garden aviaries of mixed coloured Zebra Finches. The birds themselves certainly enjoy the unhampered freedom they have when housed in flighted aviaries and reproduce very freely. Of course Zebra Finches can be kept with many other species of small Foreign Birds and they live together quite happily and many of them will breed in a mixed community. When breeding in pens I have found that Zebra Finches will breed readily in the same compartment as say a pair of Redrumps, Turquoisines, Bourke's and Cockatiels. In fact the presence of a pair of Zebra Finches in with the Parrakeets often induces both pairs to settle down to breeding more quickly.

Aviaries for accommodating Zebra Finches can be made of almost any kind of materials and small mesh wire netting. They can be large or small and of a tremendous variety of designs and may be completely new structures or older buildings suitably adapted to house the birds. All that is really needed is dry, draught-proof, well lighted, sleeping and feeding quarters, and a small mesh wire netting flight, and it is usual to have the flight approximately twice the length of the sleeping house. It is imperative that the usual precautions are taken against vermin, particularly the insertion of wire into the soil all around the outside of

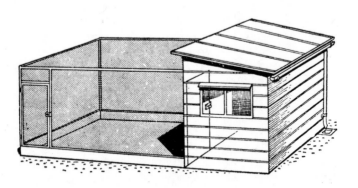

Typical form of uncontrolled aviary. When the shelter door is closed the birds can gain access to the flight through bob holes. Note the low outer door to the flight, which minimises the chances of birds escaping when the door is opened. Sometimes a safety-porch is erected as a further safeguard against such escape.

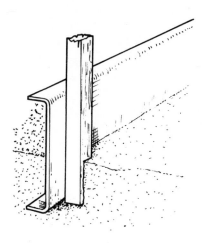

To exclude mice from an aviary, sheet metal or small mesh wire can be nailed to the uprights and turned over above and below ground level.

the flight. The floor of the flight can be concreted, covered by stone slabs, gravel, or sand, or it can be completely planted with grass. When any of these methods are used the perches can be made from natural wood branches, especially from fruit trees, and can be arranged to look most attractive. The flight of course can be planted with various bushes and shrubs such as heathers, lavender, cotoneaster, laurel, veronica, lonicera nitida, azaleas, to name a few. Frequently Zebra Finches will use the shrubs for their nesting sites where they will make their own domed nests and rear their young under completely natural conditions. If the floor of a shrub planted flight is also grassed and planted with flowering plants the aviary will look a most attractive sight with Zebra Finches flying about as in their natural habitat.

Because the restrictions on outside buildings vary

from district to district I would strongly advise Fanciers to find out from their Local Council the regulations for their area before putting up any birdroom or aviary.

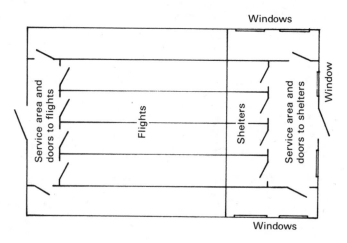

Ground plan of a range of flighted aviaries.

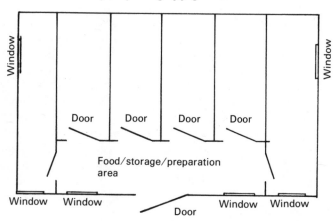

Ground plan of a range of six indoor pens.

Chapter 15

FEEDING

Zebra Finches are exceedingly easy little birds to feed under all conditions and this is a further reason for their growth in popularity amongst bird keepers. Their feeding is simple and straightforward as it consists mainly of small yellow millet, panicum as it is usually called. They will live entirely on this seed alone but it is beneficial to give them other seeds to provide a more balanced diet. A good seed mixture can be made up of four parts panicum millet, two parts plate yellow millet, one part white millet and one part small canary seed. They also like niger which is an all oil bearing seed and is particularly useful during cold weather spells but should only be given in controlled quantities because of its fattening nature. Not all Zebra Finches will at first eat canary seed and other millet seeds; however, if dishes of mixed seeds are left in their cages or aviaries they will gradually come to accept them and eat limited quantities. Japanese millet and mixed wild weed seeds can also be given as an extra variation to their diet. It is more practical to offer the birds these mixed seeds at an early age they will then eat most of them without any trouble whatsoever.

Zebra Finches like most birds of similar species are exceedingly partial to millet sprays and these are excellent for training purposes and for getting young stock to eat on their own. They can be offered to the birds in their dry state or having been soaked in clean cold water for some twenty-four hours. I like to give millet sprays dry and then I know there is no chance of them being mouldy and upsetting the stomachs of the birds. Moistened cubes of wholemeal bread are an excellent addition particularly when the pairs are rearing their chicks. Another useful food is a mixture of canary soft food (C.L.O.) and fine insectivorous food in about equal proportions. Bread and milk is also used to good effect by some breeders when the young are in the nests and when the adult birds are moulting. It is very essential that any wet food is given fresh daily, and all that which is uneaten should be removed at the end of the day. I fear that many young birds and a few adults are lost each year through consuming food which is stale or mouldy.

I find that Zebra Finches like a regular supply of various fresh green foods all through the year and particularly so at breeding times. Most breeders find that chickweed, either flowering or in its seeding state, is their favourite green food. There are other greens that are eaten quite freely and some of them can be had for each part of the year. Fresh seeding grasses which are a natural food are eaten readily by young and adult alike and supplies are generally obtainable for long periods in the year. Other green foods such as spinach, sow-thistle, shepherd's purse, tender young cabbage and dandelion leaves, chicory, lettuce, and pieces of soft sweet apple, can be given when chickweed and seeding grasses are in short supply. During the breeding period it is rather important to tie chickweed and seeding grasses into small bunches to prevent the birds from using them as nesting material. If given loose grasses Zebra Finches have a bad habit of carrying them to their nests and building on top of the clutches of eggs already there. Many nests of fertile eggs are ruined each season by the birds' zest for continual nest building.

When fresh foods are not so readily obtainable sprouted seeds will fill the gap and they provide an excellent source of nourishment. Canary, oats, wheat or millet seeds can be used for this purpose and they are quite easy to prepare. All that is necessary is to soak the chosen seeds in cold clean water in shallow pans for some twenty-four hours, then drain off the surplus water, and put the dishes of seed in a warm dark place for a few days. When the sprouts are about 3mm ($\frac{1}{8}$in) long the dishes of seeds are ready to give to the birds.

Grits and other mineral containing elements are equally necessary as good food for keeping Zebra Finches in a fine healthy condition. Most bird shops supply good quality grits of various materials such as finely crushed flint, limestone and oyster shells, that are suitable for small birds. These materials give the birds the necessary grit for grinding their food and minerals for building feather, bone and muscle. In addition to these there should always be a supply of cuttlefish bone in pieces and also crushed mineralised blocks together with crushed dried domestic hens egg shells. These latter are a very good source of calcium and will be eaten eagerly by Zebra Finches and all other seed eating birds. Sea sand, clean washed sand, old mortar rubble, and crushed chalk are other useful additions to the birds' sources of minerals. These materials are best given in separate containers.

Zebra Finches are extremely fond of bathing and as well as the supply of fresh drinking water the stock should be given separate flat dishes for bathing purposes. For small birds Zebra Finches consume a considerable amount of water and at breeding times and during hot weather it is generally necessary to inspect the water vessels twice a day.

It will be seen from the above how easy Zebra

Finches are to feed and keep in healthy condition. It is important to ensure that there is always plenty of seed in their food vessels, and not just husks, and this will mean sieving or blowing off husks and dust every time the pots are refilled. I mention this fact as I have known numbers of birds to die through lack of food although their pots were thought to have been full.

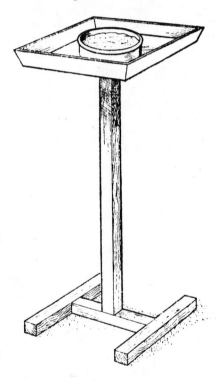

Home-made mouseproof feeding table. Some bird-keepers make this appliance with the tray inverted, but the author prefers this method as it retains the seed husks and prevents spilled seed from falling to the ground and attracting mice.

Chapter 16

THE INITIAL STOCK

Having discussed the colours, feeding and housing of
Zebra Finches in the previous Chapters I will now deal
with the stocking of a birdroom or aviary. There are
several ways in which stock can be obtained; by visiting
a local bird shop, a local Zebra Finch breeder or
through the advertisement columns of that valuable
weekly Fancy paper "Cage and Aviary Birds". When
the birds are bought locally they should be well
examined for health before a final decision is made.
Stock ordered through an advertisement from a distance
should be obtained on approval and this will give
satisfaction to both parties. Initially it is best if only one
or two colours are bought so that the first season or two
of breeding is not complicated by having many different
varieties. For this purpose I would suggest that Normal
Greys or Fawns are the best and usually the most
easy to obtain. By attending local Cage Bird Society
meetings and shows and visiting the birdrooms and
aviaries of established Fanciers a great amount of bird
knowledge can be gained. During this period of appren-
ticeship the new Fancier can be laying the foundations
of a strain. The actual forming of an individual strain
whether for colour or exhibition can be interesting,
instructive, and will encourage the breeder to do even
more with the birds.

I think that the Autumn is the best time to buy new
stock as after the breeding season the breeders have
looked over their birds and generally have a wide

choice of birds for sale. Nowadays the majority of Zebra Finch Fanciers close ring their stock and the origin of birds wearing coded rings can always be traced. When birds ringed with current year closed coded rings are bought the purchaser knows that they are young untried stock with the longest possible life expectancy. Even with fully adult birds it is best to get them with closed coded rings remembering that the breeding life of most hen Zebra Finches is about three years, the cocks a year or two more. There are of course exceptions with both sexes and I have known a few cocks fully fertile when seven to eight years old and hens at five. Nevertheless the newcomer should be content to get current year birds even though they may not look as large as some of the older ones.

I feel that I must mention the fact that no one can guarantee any particular bird or birds will breed in their new quarters. Fortunately however the vast majority of Zebra Finches will reproduce most industriously under many and varied conditions. Zebra Finches travel by rail and car exceedingly well, even for very long journeys, but a sudden change of food, housing and climate may well put them out of breeding condition for a few weeks. This being the case it is most advisable to get new stock long before they are required in the breeding quarters.

After travelling new birds should be rested in cages for a few days before they are mixed with the existing stock. This will give the birds a chance to recover from their travels and settle down to the change of environment and management. This caging also gives the new owner an opportunity to study them at close quarters and to see if they are what is required to add to or strengthen the stock. Providing the new birds are active, alert and bright eyed a few missing or broken feathers can be discounted as they will automatically be re-placed in course of time. Should the birds be required for exhibition the missing claws or bent toes are import-ant features as they are show faults but of course do not hamper the birds from breeding.

The breeder should not be too disappointed if the new stock does not commence to breed right away even though they may look very fit. Some birds take much longer than others to settle down in new surroundings and again there is a difference in the time it takes for individual birds to become fully mature. It can be most useful to take note when particular birds develop full maturity and start to breed. This information will serve as a guide to the owner when matching up the pairs for breeding. Newcomers to the Zebra Finch Fancy must recognise the fact that with the breeding of livestock there will always be deaths and breeding failures amongst the stock. Once these facts are accepted the breeder will have a much better under-standing of the birds and their limitations.

Pair of Normal Grey Penguin Zebra Finches on their nest box.

Chapter 17

BREEDING PROCEDURE

Individual owners of Zebra Finches have their own particular methods of breeding procedure which they find suit their own stock of birds. Most of these steps taken will of course be the same but it is the small details which may differ. In this chapter I will be discussing the principle of the breeding method used by the majority of Zebra Finch keepers leaving the minor points to their own circumstances.

Having set up the housing and obtained the necessary stock of birds plans for the breeding season will be uppermost in the minds of the fanciers. No birds should be considered for breeding unless they are in a robust physical condition. Should either or both members of selected pairs not be fully ready for the task their mating will not be successful; even if eggs are laid and chicks hatched they are likely to be weakly, poor quality, and more often than not die quickly. In some instances the clutches of eggs will be infertile and quite frequently the hens fail to lay at all.

It is really quite easy to see when the birds are ready for breeding even if it is the owner's first season. Cock birds in full breeding condition look aggressively alert and strongly inclined to pick quarrels with each other, call to nearby hens, and execute their funny little neck stretching courtship display. Hen birds also get quarrelsome and look for possible nesting sites often with a feather or a piece of grass in their beaks, calling to the cocks at the same time. When two birds are seen to be in this high condition they can be safely mated, usually with excellent results providing the breeding quarters and prevailing weather conditions are suitable.

One of the most frequently voiced questions by new breeders is when is the right time to start off breeding operations. Experienced Fanciers have their own ideas on when to start but for the beginner I would suggest that the end of February to the beginning of March is the most suitable period. At that time of year the hours of daylight are lengthening, the days are warmer, and there is more availability of green food, all of which helps to make breeding successful. If the breeder should be tempted to commence too soon there is always the possibility of hens getting egg bound, eggs getting chilled, or chicks being deserted if the weather conditions are too cold. I have always noticed that when there is more warm sunlight Zebra Finches breed better, more eggs hatch, and a greater number of healthy chicks are reared per nest. To my way of thinking it is far better to make haste slowly when dealing with the breeding of birds of all kinds.

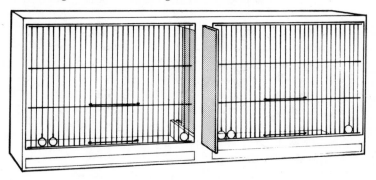

A double breeder stock cage, with central partition extended. Fully removed the two cages make a nice small flight cage.

Any birds that have been housed in stock cages for show purposes for any length of time will do much better when nesting if they are first given some weeks of freedom in a large flight. Plenty of flying exercise is an excellent way of toning up the birds' muscular systems ready for breeding. The addition of a little soft food and extra green food is also helpful when given for a few weeks prior to mating time. Undoubtedly the best way to keep breeding stock at all times except when they are actually nesting is outdoor flighted aviaries with the sexes apart. This ideal is not possible for all breeders and good long flight cages or pens make very good substitutes for giving the birds their needed exercise.

Pair of Penguin Zebra Finches nesting in a cage with the hen about to lay her eggs.

When using single pair cages or pens for breeding only one nest box will be needed for each pair. Where two or more pairs are together then more nest boxes than pairs must be given to prevent the birds fighting as they surely will if they have not enough choice. When the pairs have made their selection and started to build the unused boxes can, if the owner wishes, be removed and used when changes are needed. Zebra Finches on the whole are most accommodating little birds and will build their nests almost anywhere and in any receptacle. Some inspections of the nests are needed and for this purpose the wooden type nest boxes are the most practical; the best kind of nest boxes are 13cm (5in) wooden cubes, with a hinged inspection lid and a half open front for entrance. Boxes that are completely

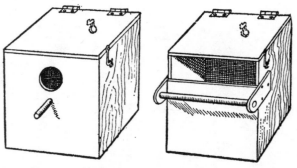

Nesting boxes for Zebra Finches.

enclosed or woven wicker nest baskets are sometimes used but they prevent the necessary inspections. On the whole Zebra Finches do not mind their owners having a periodic peep into their nests to see the eggs or ring the chicks. Although this may be so I would advise new breeders to refrain from making too many inspections as these are likely to annoy the parent birds and could cause them to desert their chicks. I think the best time for looking at the nest boxes is during the birds' first feeding time of the day as if they are disturbed then they have plenty of time to settle down before the owner's next visit.

When Zebra Finches are being bred in cages many of them have a tendency to pop in and out of their nest boxes when they see the owner entering the birdroom and often to the detriment of the eggs. To help to prevent this from happening and to give the pairs a certain amount of privacy a piece of carboard should be fixed onto the wire front opposite the nest box. I have tried this out myself and found it has a most pacifying effect on the birds.

Before hanging up the nest boxes I always half fill them with soft dried grasses so that the birds have something on which to build their nests. They will also need a further supply of these dried grasses and a few soft feathers to complete their nest building operations. Once the eggs have started to appear all unused nesting material should be removed to prevent continual building ending in "sandwich" nests. The amount of nesting material given can easily be controlled in cages and pens but in larger aviaries it is much more difficult. Strangely enough when breeding in aviaries Zebra Finches seem far less likely to build "sandwich" nests than they do in other breeding quarters. It is most likely the extra amount of flying space they have accounts for this.

The usual clutches of eggs laid by Zebra Finches are four or five per nest although some prolific hens will produce up to ten in a single clutch. The incubation period is about twelve days and is shared by both parents as also is the feeding of their chicks. Incubation will start off after the second or third egg of a clutch

Zebra Finch nest, made of soft grass and feathers, containing six eggs.

has been laid and this means there can be a few days difference between the hatching of the first and last chicks. This does not seem to bother the parent birds in the least and they tend each baby with equal care. Most Zebra Finch pairs make first rate parents and look after their broods extremely well right through until they can fully fend for themselves. With this good attention the young birds develop rapidly and are usually ready to leave their nest boxes when between sixteen to eighteen days old. After they have flown the adult birds feed them for a further seven to ten days. I have noticed they always develop quicker in the warmer weather than they do when it is cold and damp. Immediately the young birds are seen to be feeding well on their own they should be taken from their parents so that the adult birds can nest again un-hampered. If the chicks are not removed there is always a possibility if they still frequent the nest box of the

A Fawn hen eating soft food prior to feeding her waiting chick.

The hen must retain the food long enough for it to reach her body temperature before passing it to her chick.

The food is pushed in at all angles—as long as enough goes in the chick does not mind how.

adults attacking them quite fiercely. This is more likely to occur in cages but even in aviaries the young are far safer if removed from their parents.

Ringing

It is the accepted practice amongst the majority of Zebra Finch breeders to close ring the young birds with coded metal rings. Such rings are issued to members through The Zebra Finch Society or one of its Area Societies where each member is allocated a special code number of his own. The non-coded year dated and numbered metal closed rings can be obtained by non Society members from Messrs Hughes, 1, High Street, Hampton Hill, Middlesex. Celluloid coloured split rings are also used quite extensively by breeders to mark birds from different pairs and they are most useful for identifying birds without actually having to catch them and for marking show pairs.

When the feet and legs of baby Zebra Finches are seen for the first time the owner may wonder how it is possible to close ring such tiny fragile looking chicks. Of course great care must be taken when putting on rings not to handle the youngsters too strongly. However the chicks are quite tough little birds and once the owner has got over the first shock of handling such tiny things their ringing becomes relatively simple. This is borne out by the fact that tens of thousands of closed rings are issued each year through the various Zebra Finch Societies.

There are two schools of thought as to the best age for ringing young Zebra Finches, some like to put them on when the babies are still quite small and others like myself prefer to ring when they are just starting to shoot their feathers. The reason I like the older birds is they are easier to handle, being larger, and also there is less chance of the rings slipping off or riding up over the knee joint. I would advise newcomers to try out both methods to find out which really suits them better. If the owner starts to close ring the chicks in the first breeding season there is every chance that it will be carried out successfully even if the odd birds are missed here and there.

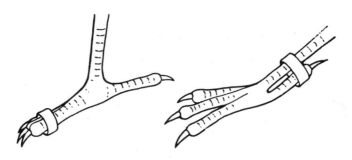

The correct way to ring a young bird.

It is relatively simple to close ring young Zebra Finches by holding a chick gently but firmly in the hand with one of the legs taken between the forefinger and thumb. The ring is then put over the three longest toes, up and along the leg, and the short back toe is then pulled through the ring with the aid of a sharpened matchstick or something similar. Although a chick may squeak a little it is from indignation of being handled and not because it is being hurt. For the first few times the owner may be somewhat apprehensive but after that it is only a matter of seconds for a closed ring to be slipped over the chick's leg.

Split coloured celluloid rings are usually put on after the birds have left the nest boxes and I do this when the chicks are first taken from their parents and move to the young bird quarters. The colour of the celluloid rings used for each nest should be entered in the stock register against the appropriate pair at the time of ringing. I also find young birds are best kept in flights with the sexes apart as it is possible to sex them when only a few weeks old. In fact all Zebra Finches both adult and young should be kept in flights with the sexes apart except when they are required for breeding or being trained for exhibition. This prevents indiscriminate matings, fighting, and unwanted egg laying and the birds pair more readily when given their partners chosen by the breeder.

An important part of bird breeding is the keeping of a breeding register so that the ancestry and other relevant details of the stock are recorded. There are numerous styles in which such a book can be kept and each breeder will in time devise his own special method. The items that must be recorded are the pedigrees, age, colour, and ring number of each stock bird, the different pairings made each year and the young they produce together with the ring numbers. Other items such as breeding peculiarities of particular birds, unexplained colour results, and any show awards, can also be entered in the register. When breeding for colour is being carried out it will quickly be realised the importance of an accurate breeding register. Young birds from one nest should not be moved to another until the chicks are rung and entered in the register as if this is not done unsatisfactory pairings in later years can be carried out to the detriment of the whole stock.

New breeders of Zebra Finches are often very surprised and somewhat puzzled by the colour of the beaks of young birds differing so considerably from those of the adults. When young Normal Grey, Silver and other dark coloured Zebra Finches leave their nest boxes their beaks are black; those of Fawns, Creams

BREEDING REGISTER

PAIR (or CAGE) No. ....   **COCK** ....   **HEN** ....

Date Hen is set.	Date due to Hatch	Number of eggs.	Number of young.	Remarks	Description of Young, with Ring Numbers or distinguishing marks (if any)

PAIR (or CAGE) No. ....   **COCK** ....   **HEN** ....

The cage number will be entered from the label on the breeding cage, together with the name, or number, of the cock and hen (obtained from the Pedigree Register). The date under HEN SET should be that on which the first egg is laid. DUE TO HATCH indicates the fourteenth day from the date the hen was set. REMARKS: Under this heading infertile or broken eggs, dead chicks, etc., should be recorded.

etc. are brownish; and those of Whites and Chestnut-flanked Whites are whitish horn coloured. After they have been out of their boxes for a week or two their beaks start to change to the well known shades of coral red (excepting the yellow-beaked varieties which change to shades of orange yellow).

During the course of this chapter I have dealt with the breeding of Zebra Finches from the time the eggs hatch until the fully grown young birds leave the care of their parents. I will list the particulars of the various breeding combinations and give examples of how the characters are inherited.

Sex-linked inheritance

P.1 Sex-linked cock × Normal hen
F.1 Normal/Sex-linked cocks × Sex-linked hens
F.2 Sex-linked cocks   Normal hens
     Normal/Sex-linked cocks   Sex-linked hens.

Example: Fawn cock × Normal hen produces Normal/Fawn cocks and Fawn hens.

Dominant inheritance

P.1 Dominant single character cock × Normal hen
F.1 Normal cocks   Normal hens
     Dominant single character cocks × Dominant
                                  single character hens
F.2 Dominant double character   Dominant single
                                               character
     Normal   Cocks and Hens   Dominant single
                                               character

Example: Silver single character cock × Silver single character hen produces Silver double character, Silver single character and Normal cocks and hens.

Recessive inheritance

P.1 Recessive cock × Normal hen

F.1 Normal/Recessive cocks × Normal/Recessive hens

F.2 Recessive   Normal/Recessive
    Normal   Cocks and Hens   Normal/Recessive

Example: Normal cock × Pied hen produces all Normal/Pied cocks and hens.

By using these examples and substituting various colours all mating results can be calculated and as a further help to breeders some theoretical expectations of the various colours will be found in Appendix 2.

Sex-linked inheritance

1. Sex-linked cock × Sex-linked hen
   50 % Sex-linked cocks   50 % Sex-linked hens.

2. Sex-linked cock × Non-linked hen
   50 % Non-linked/Sex-linked cocks   50 % Sex-linked hens.

3. Non-linked cock × Sex-linked hen
   50 % Non-linked/Sex-linked cocks   50 % Non-linked hens.

4. Non-linked/Sex-linked cock × Non-linked hen
   25 % Non-linked/Sex-linked cocks   25 % Non-linked cocks   25 % Sex-linked hens   25 % Non-linked hens.

5. Non-linked/Sex-linked cock × Sex-linked hen
   25 % Sex-linked cocks   25 % Sex-linked hens
   25 % Non-linked/Sex-linked cocks   25 % Non-linked hens.

Chapter 18

SHOWING PROCEDURE

After keeping and breeding Zebra Finches for a time many Fanciers feel they would like to enter their birds at a show. Shows for cage and aviary birds are held all over the country and there is usually at least one show in every reasonably sized town. Zebra Finches make ideal subjects for exhibiting as they are quite easy to train for show work, travel well by road or rail, and the classification for them at shows is good. One of the satisfactions of exhibiting is when the birds bred by the owner score a success indicating that the breeding programme has been correct.

Exhibiting means a lot more than just having and breeding good shapely birds and putting them into show cages and taking them to a show. Exhibition stock of all kinds have to be given a period of training so that they will display to advantage their good points before the judge. Some birds have a natural bent for show work and a few are untrainable but the majority need only a week or so of preparation before they are quite happy in show cages.

It should always be remembered that Zebra Finches of all the different colour mutations are domesticated and NOT Foreign birds and therefore cannot compete in Foreign Bird classes or for their special prizes. Zebra Finches must always be exhibited in true pairs of the same colour at shows where Patronage of the Z.F.S. or its Area Societies has been given. There is a difference between show pairs which must be of the same colour and can be closely related and breeding pairs where the colours may be mixed and the relationship must not be too close.

The first step in the preparation of exhibition birds is to select from the stock the pairs that are to be shown. Care must be taken in picking out matching pairs of the same colour shade, shape, size, feather quality, with all claws and toes complete. These birds should then be put into stock cages either in single true pairs or in separate sexes about four birds per cage. Zebra Finches that have been bred in cages will naturally require less time to steady down than those caught up from pens or aviaries. When the owner is quite sure that the birds are happy in their stock cages training show cages can then be hung over the open stock cage doors. At first to encourage the birds to enter pieces of millet spray or some of their favourite green food should be put into the training cage. After the birds have become used to going in and out the pairs can be shut in for an hour or two at first, gradually increasing the time until they are in all day. When they have been in show cages a number of times and have settled down to the more confined space they are ready for showing. However, before they are actually sent to a show they should be moved about and perhaps taken into the house occasionally so they get accustomed to their cages being moved and handled.

It is always advisable to have more birds caged than those actually required for any show to provide substitutes should a bird go soft or lose some feathers in a noticeable place. When a replacement is made care should be taken to ensure that the newly made up pair match each other in all respects. The following is The Zebra Finch Society's guidance for show standards.

Show Standards

Condition to be essential. Birds should not receive any award unless in perfect show condition. (Missing, ragged or soiled feathers, and missing claws or toes constitute show faults.)

Type. Bold throughout and of the "Cobby" type, giving the birds a look of substance; wings evenly carried to root of tail.

Markings (Cocks). Chest bar distinct and clear cut, *not less* than ⅛in wide and of even width throughout. Side flankings should be prominent, extending from wing butts to end of rump and decorated with round, clearly defined white spots. Beak coral red with feet and legs deep pink. All markings where applicable to be clear and distinct. Hens as for cocks less cheek patches, chest bar and side flankings; beak a paler shade of red. Male markings on hens are definite show faults.

When showing at Zebra Finch Society and Area Society Patronage shows the birds competing for these Specialist Societies special prizes and other awards must always be shown in standard show cages. These show cages can be made by the exhibitor or can be bought from cage manufacturing firms, but wherever they are made they must be of the exact Zebra Finch Society specification.

Standard Show Cage Specification

SIZE. Overall measurement: 305mm (12in) long, 298mm (11¾in) high, 152mm (6in) deep.

WOOD. Top, sides and false roof. Back good quality 4mm (⅛in) ply.

DOOR. Round. 89mm (3½in) dia. Centre 137mm (5⅜in) from floor of cage. Centred on depth, one wire loop.

FRONT RAIL. Height 60mm (2⅜in) from floor, turn out feeder door on left hand side of front rail 89mm (3½in) long by 35mm (1⅜in) deep; sloping cut at edge. 16-gauge escape bar fixed to door. Door fastened by 22mm (⅞in) brass desk turn painted black. Zinc clip screwed to inside of door to carry white plastic drinker, 19mm (¾in) 16-gauge S-hook on outside.
PERCHES. Length 102mm (4in) overall measured from

THE ZEBRA FINCH SOCIETY STANDARD SHOW CAGE

the back of the cage, 10mm ($\frac{3}{8}$in) diameter with plain boss at back 25mm (1in) diameter projecting 10mm ($\frac{3}{8}$in). Perches to be fixed 114mm ($4\frac{1}{2}$in) from floor of cage and 102mm (4in) apart on the centre line of the cage horizontally.

WIRE FRONT. Comprising 23 wires, 16-gauge mesh, 13mm ($\frac{1}{2}$in) centre to centre, double punched bar at top set 5mm ($\frac{3}{16}$in) apart, for fixing two wires left at top and bottom.

TOP. Width 133mm ($5\frac{1}{4}$in). Carrying hole 32mm ($1\frac{1}{4}$in) dia., centre 35mm ($1\frac{3}{8}$in) from back of cage.

COLOUR. Inside painted white, outside and wire front black.

Floor covering—small Yellow Millet or any suitable seed mixture.

NO MAKERS NAME TO APPEAR ON CAGE.

Prior to the chosen pairs being sent to a show they will be required to be entered in their proper classes at that show. A schedule of classes and entry forms can be obtained from the Secretary of the Show Promoting Society. The entry form should be filled up in detail and returned to the Secretary together with the necessary entrance fees well before the closing date for entries. In due course the exhibitor will receive back the class labels which should be stuck in the centre of the bottom rails of the show cages. Before taking or sending birds to the show a check should be made on the cages to see that they have the correct cage labels for the birds inside. The show schedules must be carefully read for the times of delivery and collection and any other important points regarding the show.

Lists of shows that are held in various parts of the country over the show season will be published periodically in "Cage and Aviary Birds". Members of Specialist Zebra Finch Societies will be notified in their publications of all the Patronage Zebra Finch shows. I would wish all new exhibitors success with their endeavours and ask them not to be too disappointed if they do not win with their birds on the first effort. If they proceed on the right lines they will in the end be successful.

SHOW REGISTER

Name of Show.	Date.	No. of Entries	Judge or Judges.	Cards Won.	Total Cash Prizes and Value	Specials Won.	Date Prizes Received.	Expenses.			Performances of Birds and Other Remarks.

Chapter 19

FIRST AID TREATMENT

Colds and chills

When strong well bred and well fed Zebra Finches are housed in good dry, draught proof quarters, there will be little risk of them contracting colds or chills. However it can happen at odd times that a bird gets a little off colour and as soon as it is noticed sitting fluffed up it should be put into a small cage and taken into a warm temperature of (20°–27°C). 70°–80°F.

In most instances if the patients are caught in time a few days in a warm room will quickly cure the condition. If any bird does not seem to be making progress to recovery after a day or two Dianimol syrup or Syrup of Buckthorn should be added to the drinking water, about five drops to a tablespoonful of water.

Sick birds often need a little tempting to eat and in addition to their seed they should be offered millet sprays, tepid water sweetened with glucose and warm wholemeal bread and milk, but no green food. When a bird has recovered it should gradually be hardened off before being allowed back to the birdroom or aviary. If a bird is returned too quickly it could easily result in a relapse which could be fatal. When a sick bird has been handled it is most important for the owner to thoroughly wash before touching any other birds or their food. Any cage or feeding utensils that have been used for a sick bird must be thoroughly disinfected before being used again.

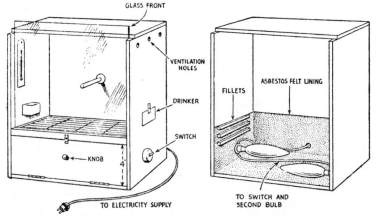

A glass-fronted hospital cage with exposed heating arrangements. The author prefers the perch a little lower and across the cage rather than from back to front.

Damage to wing or leg

It is not easy to do much for a damaged wing without causing further complications except to place the bird in a small cage with plenty of food, grit and water, and leave it in a quiet place so that the damage can heal on its own. In most cases a wing will heal quite well even if not quite in its normal position and flying will be possible.

A broken leg can be set and carefully splinted with either a section of a large quill feather or a piece of matchwood. It requires two people to do this and great care must be taken that more damage is not done whilst putting on the splint. After this is done two or three weeks caged on its own is usually time for the bone to knit and the bird can be returned to its original cage.

Diarrhoea

In the early stages treat as for colds and chills, but in

longer standing cases Sulphamethazine 16% solution should be used instead of Dianimol syrup or Syrup of Buckthorn. This should be given for three days, then three days missed, and then given for one further day. The dosage is four drops to a tablespoonful of water that has first been boiled.

The usual disinfecting of cages, seed and water vessels, is of paramount importance when dealing with a sickness of this nature.

Enteritis
If neglected Diarrhoea can develop into the more serious condition of Enteritis and is much more difficult to treat. Enteritis can be contagious and therefore every effort must be taken to prevent the condition from spreading in the stock. Everything that has been in contact with a sick bird must be thoroughly disinfected and the owner must wash both before and after treating the patient.

The initial treatment is as for colds but with the use of Sulphamethazine 16% solution which should be given for four days and then three days missed and then given for two further days. The dosage is four drops to a tablespoonful of water that has first been boiled. Even warmth is essential both day and night to help to maintain the body heat. When a bird has recovered it will need several weeks of rest before being returned to its normal surroundings.

Egg binding
During the early part of the year Zebra Finch hens are more likely to fall victims of egg binding because of the cold, wet and windy weather conditions that usually prevail. Undoubtedly the best prevention against this trouble is to refrain from breeding too early in the year

and use only fully adult birds that have been well fed, had access to ample supplies of grits and other minerals, and the opportunity of plenty of flying exercise. Should a hen be seen sitting in a huddled position with feathers rumpled breathing heavily and swollen at the vent she is suffering from egg binding. Such a bird should be gently caught and put into a small cage (or hospital cage) and taken into a very warm room. After a few hours of heat which will loosen the muscle tension a bird will generally pass an egg. A few drops of glycerine or a mixture of gin and glycerine in the drinking water will also have a beneficial effect on a sick bird. When the egg has been laid the bird will need to be kept warm for a few further days before being hardened off. It is unwise to use a hen that has been egg bound and recovered for further breeding until after she has had a few weeks rest in a flight.

Over-grown claws and beaks
When small active birds like Zebra Finches are housed in somewhat confined quarters there is always the likeli-

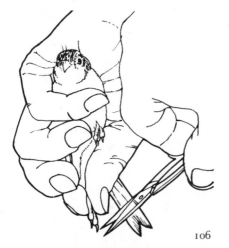

The correct way to trim a bird's nails.

hood of their toenails becoming overlong. If these are not clipped eggs may get spoiled at breeding times and the birds themselves would be penalised at shows. As it will have been seen, the toenails of Zebra Finches are quite fine and care must be exercised when they are being cut. If the nails are closely examined a small blood vessel will be seen running part way down each nail. The cuts should be made just before the end of the vein. Should a vein be accidentally cut a spot of tincture of iodine or T.C.P. will stop infection.

Sometimes the top part of the beak will over-grow and need trimming to normal length. With the aid of a sharp pair of small scissors the surplus growth should be gently clipped away. Here again care must be taken that the blood vessels are not cut.

Sores on feet

Zebra Finches and similar small birds when confined to cages can develop sore patches on their feet. These sores are mostly caused by fine pieces of grit or small seed husks getting stuck to the feet by moist droppings forming into hard lumps which become infected. When a bird is noticed with a sore foot it should be caught and put into a clean cage on its own. The foot should be bathed in Dettol and warm water to soften the lump so that it will crumble away. After this has been done and the foot dried the sore should be dusted with antiseptic powder and the bird kept caged until the sore has healed. Perches of various thicknesses both in cage and aviary will help to keep the feet supple and therefore less likely to get sores.

Strokes

If a bird suddenly dies the cause is usually a stroke for which there are no warning symptoms and nothing can be done to prevent its occurrence. Sometimes a stroke is less severe and the bird is only partially affected, losing some use of wing or leg. A bird found in such a condition should be caged on its own and kept in a quiet place. It usually takes a few weeks for a bird to get back into its normal health. When birds are in a high condition at breeding time and then get over excited it is always possible for a stroke to happen. This is the reason why birds in apparent perfect health and feather sometimes are unexpectedly found dead.

I would suggest that the new breeder when finding sickness amongst the stock which cannot be understood should contact the nearest experienced cage bird breeder for advice.

Appendix 1

ZEBRA FINCH SOCIETIES

The Zebra Finch Society, Secretary: J. A. W. Prior, 103, Horncastle Road, Lee, London, SE12 9LF.

The Midland Zebra Finch Club, Secretary: M. S. Wrenn, Clapgate Lane, Bartley Green, Birmingham.

South Western Zebra Finch Club, Secretary: W. J. C. Hocking, 16, Illogan Park, Illogan, Redruth, Cornwall.

Scottish and Northern Counties Zebra Finch Society, Secretary: J. R. Addison, 33, Grinsdale Avenue, Bell Vue, Carlisle.

The Kent Zebra Finch Club, Secretary: E. D. Barlow, 64, Manor Park Road, West Wickham, Kent.

The Scottish Zebra Finch Society, Secretary: D. Liddle, 48, Edinburgh Road, Penicuick, Midlothean, Scotland.

The East Anglian Zebra Finch Society, Secretary: Mrs. Y. Stanhope, 1, Euston Avenue, Hawthorn Bank, Spalding, Lincs. PE11 2UX.

The Yorkshire and Allied Counties Zebra Finch Society, Secretary: L. T. Holmes, 6, Queens Crescent, Edlington, Doncaster, Yorkshire.

Irish Zebra Finch Society, Secretary: L. Cassidy, 43, Eden Villas, Dun Laoghaire, Co. Dublin, Ireland.

The Zebra Finch Society of Australia, Secretary: K. W. Plimmer, 24, Ryvie Avenue, Cromer, 2099, N.S.W., Australia.

The Zebra Finch Society of America, Secretary: D. W. Seabury, 8204, Woodland Avenue, Annandale, Virginia, 22003 U.S.A.

Austauschzentrale der Exoten-Liebhaber und Zeuchter,
   H. Potzke, 3001, Rsernhagen 13, Ostprenpenweb 10,
   Germany.
Dansk Zebrafinke Opdraetter Klub, Ellen Andreasen,
   Fasanvei 13, 7000 Roskilde, Denmark.
Nederlandse Zebravinken Club, B.L.v.d. Stroom, Mgr,
   Dr. H. Poelslaan, 1, Amstelveen-Bovenkerk, Holland.

A SELECTION OF ZEBRA FINCH MATING EXPECTATIONS

Normal Grey × Normal Grey	100% Normal Grey.
Normal Grey × Normal White	100% Normal Grey/White.
Normal Grey × Normal Pied	100% Normal Grey/Pied.
Normal Grey × Normal Penguin	100% Normal Grey/Penguin.
Normal Grey × Normal Grey Yellow-beak	100% Normal Grey/Yellow-beak.
Normal White × Normal Pied	100% Normal Grey/Pied White.
Normal White × Penguin	100% Normal Grey/Penguin.
Penguin × Pied	100% Normal Grey/Penguin Pied.
Fawn cock × Normal Grey hen	50% Normal Grey/Fawn cocks and 50% Fawn hens.
Normal Grey/Fawn cock × Fawn hen	25% Fawn cocks, 25% Fawn hens, 25% Normal Grey/Fawn cocks and 25% Normal Grey hens.
Fawn cock × Normal Grey Yellow-beak hen	50% Normal Grey/Fawn Yellow-beak cocks, 50% Fawn/Yellow-beak hens.
Normal Grey Yellow-beak cock × Fawn hen	50% Normal Grey/Fawn Yellow-beak cocks, 50% Normal Grey/Yellow-beak hens.

Fawn cock × White hen — 50 % Grey/Fawn White cocks, 50 % Fawn/White hens.

White cock × Fawn hen — 50 % Grey/Fawn White cocks, 50 % Grey White hens.

Fawn cock × Pied hen — 50 % Grey/Fawn Pied cocks, 50 % Fawn/Pied hens.

Pied cock × Fawn hen — 50 % Grey/Fawn Pied cocks, 50 % Grey/Pied hens.

Fawn cock × Penguin hen — 50 % Grey/Fawn Penguin cocks, 50 % Fawn/Penguin hens.

Penguin cock × Fawn hen — 50 % Grey/Fawn Penguin cocks, 50 % Grey/Penguin hens.

Chestnut-flanked White cock × Grey hen — 50 % Grey/Chestnut-flanked White cocks, 50 % Chestnut-flanked White hens.

Grey cock × Chestnut-flanked White hen — 50 % Grey/Chestnut-flanked White cocks, 50 % Grey hens.

White cock × Chestnut-flanked White hen — 50 % Grey/Chestnut-flanked White and White cocks, 50 % Grey/White hens.

Chestnut-flanked White cock × White hen — 50 % Grey/Chestnut-flanked White and White cocks, 50 % Chestnut-flanked White/White hens.

Chestnut-flanked White cock × Pied hen	50 % Grey/Chestnut-flanked White Pied cocks, 50 % Chestnut-flanked White/Pied hens.
Pied cock × Chestnut-flanked White hen	50 % Grey/Chestnut-flanked White Pied cocks, 50 % Grey/Pied hens.
Chestnut-flanked White cock × Penguin hen	50 % Grey/Chestnut-flanked Penguin cocks, 50 % Chestnut-flanked White/Penguin hens.
Penguin cock × Chestnut-flanked White hen	50 % Grey/Chestnut-flanked White Penguin cocks, 50 % Grey/Penguin hens.
Normal Grey ×Silver single factor	50 % Normal Grey, 50 % Silver single factor.
White ×Silver single factor	50 % Normal Grey/White, 50 % Silver single factor/White.
Pied ×Silver single factor	50 % Normal Grey/Pied, 50 % Silver single factor/Pied.
Penguin ×Silver single factor	50 % Normal Grey/Penguin, 50 % Silver single factor/Penguin.
Fawn cock ×Silver single factor hen	25 % Grey/Fawn cocks, 25 % Silver single factor/Fawn cocks, 25 % Fawn hens, 25 % Cream single factor hens.
Silver single factor cock ×Fawn hen	25 % Grey/Fawn cocks, 25 % Silver single factor/Fawn cocks, 25 % Grey hens, 25 % Silver single factor hens.

Cream single factor cock × Silver double factor hen

25% Silver double factor/Cream cocks, 25% Silver single factor/Cream cocks, 25% Cream double factor hens, 25% Cream single factor hens.

Cream single factor cock × White hen

25% Grey/Fawn White cocks, 25% Silver single factor/Cream White cocks, 25% Fawn/White hens, single factor 25% Cream White hens.

White cock × Cream single factor hen

25% Grey/Fawn White cocks, 25% Silver single factor/Cream White cocks, 25% Grey/White hens, 25% Silver single factor/White hens.

Cream single factor cock × Pied hen

25% Grey/Fawn Pied cocks, 25% Silver single factor/Cream Pied cocks, 25% Fawn/Pied hens, 25% Cream single factor/Pied hens.

Pied cock × Cream single factor hen

25% Grey/Fawn Pied cocks, 25% Silver single factor/Cream Pied cocks, 25% Grey/Pied hens, 25% Silver single factor/Pied hens.

Cream single factor cock × Penguin hen

25% Grey/Fawn Penguin cocks, 25% Silver single factor/Cream Penguin cocks, 25% Fawn/Penguin hens, 25% Cream single factor/Penguin hens.

Penguin cock × Cream single factor hen

25 % Grey/Fawn Penguin cocks, 25 % Silver single factor/Cream Penguin cocks, 25 % Grey/Penguin hens, 25 % Silver single factor/Penguin hens.

Cream single factor cock × Chestnut-flanked White hen

25 % Grey/Fawn Chestnut-flanked White cocks, 25 % Silver single factor/Cream Chestnut-flanked White cocks, 25 % Fawn hens, 25 % Cream single factor hens.

Chestnut-flanked White cock × Cream single factor hen

25 % Grey/Fawn Chestnut-flanked White cocks, 25 % Silver single factor/Cream Chestnut-flanked White cocks, 25 % Chestnut-flanked White hens, 25 % Silver Chestnut-flanked White hens, 25 % Silver single factor Chestnut-flanked White hens.

Grey/Penguin × Grey/Penguin

25 % Grey, 50 % Grey/Penguin, 25 % Penguin.

Grey/Penguin × Grey

50 % Grey, 50 % Grey/Penguin.

Grey/Penguin × Fawn hen

25 % Grey hens, 25 % Grey/Penguin hens, 25 % Grey/Fawn cocks, 25 % Grey/Fawn Penguin cocks.

Grey/Penguin × Fawn cock

25 % Fawn hens, 25 % Fawn/Penguin hens, 25 % Grey/Fawn cocks, 25 % Grey/Fawn Penguin cocks.

Grey/Penguin × Fawn/Penguin hen

$12\frac{1}{2}\%$ Grey hens, 25% Grey/Penguin hens, $12\frac{1}{2}\%$ Penguin hens, $12\frac{1}{2}\%$ Grey/Fawn cocks, 25% Grey/Penguin Fawn cocks, $12\frac{1}{2}\%$ Penguin/Fawn cocks.

Grey/Penguin × Fawn/Penguin cock

$12\frac{1}{2}\%$ Fawn hens, 25% Fawn/Penguin hens, $12\frac{1}{2}\%$ Fawn Penguin hens, $12\frac{1}{2}\%$ Grey/ Fawn cocks, 25% Grey/Fawn Penguin cocks, $12\frac{1}{2}\%$ Penguin/Fawn cocks.

Grey/Chestnut-flanked White cock × Chestnut-flanked White hen

25% Grey/Chestnut-flanked White cocks, 25% Chestnut-flanked White cocks, 25% Chestnut-flanked White hens, 25% Grey hens.

Grey/Chestnut-flanked White cock × Grey hen

25% Chestnut-flanked White hens, 25% Grey hens, 25% Grey cocks, 25% Grey/ Chestnut-flanked White cocks.

Grey/Chestnut-flanked White cock × Pied hen

25% Chestnut-flanked White/Pied hens, 25% Grey/Pied hens, 25% Grey/Pied cocks, 25% Grey/Chestnut-flanked Pied cocks.

BIBLIOGRAPHY

YOUR ZEBRA FINCH, *K. Lawrence, Photo-Precision*.

ZEBRA FINCHES, *C. H. Rogers, 2nd Ed., K. & R. Books Ltd., (Now out of print)*

FOREIGN BIRDS IN COLOUR, *Vol. x, A. Rutgers, Blandford Press*

FINCHES & SOFTBILLED BIRDS, *H. Bates/H. Busenbark, TFH, Pub.*

ENCYCLOPAEDIA OF AVICULTURE VOL. 3, *A. Rutgers, Blandford Press*

FOREIGN BIRDS FOR BEGINNERS, *D. H. Risdon, Iliffe/K & R Books*

AVIARY BIRDS IN COLOUR, *D. Avon/T. Tilford, Blandford Press*

ENCYCLOPAEDIA OF CAGE & AVIARY BIRDS, *C. H. Rogers, Pelham Books*

FOREIGN BIRDKEEPING, *E. Boosey, Iliffe Books, (Now out of print)*

DICTIONARY OF BIRDS IN COLOUR, *Campbell, B., Michael Joseph*

YOUR BIRD, *D. Kelsey-Wood, Photo-Precision*

AUSTRALIAN FINCHES, *C. Immelman, Angus & Robertson*

WHAT BIRD IS THAT, *A guide to the birds of Australia, N. W. Cayley, Angus & Robertson*

The above books are available from all leading booksellers and pet stores. Where titles are out of print, antiquarian and second-hand bookstores may have copies.

GLOSSARY

ALBINO. A red-eyed mutation where all dark pigments are absent from the plumage.

CHARACTER. The special genes on which the colour determining bodies are carried.

CHEEK LOBES. The area on the cheeks covering the ears.

CHEST BAR. The wide dark bar below the zebra markings on a cock's chest.

CLUTCH. The nest of eggs laid by a hen in a sitting.

COBBY. Short well-rounded body.

COUNTERPART. A colour mutation which is similar to the Normal.

CREST-BRED. A non-crested bird produced from one Crested parent.

CRESTED. A bird with a definite head crest.

DILUTE. A plumage colouring that is less in colour depth than the Normal.

DOMESTICATED. A species that has been bred for many generations under captive conditions.

DOMINANT. A colour or other feature that dominates other colours.

DOUBLE CHARACTER. A bird having the same character on both of its chromosomes.

FLANK MARKINGS. The white spotted coloured markings on each side.

FLIGHT FEATHERS. The longest feathers in the wings.

GENETIC MAKE-UP. The characters possessed by a bird that can be inherited.

GRIZZLED. A mixture of light and dark areas on the same feathers that give a pepper and salt effect.

LACING. A lighter colour pencilling on a dark ground.

LETHAL. A character that destroys the chicks just before or just as they are hatched.

MUTATION. A sudden change in a colour character.

OUTCROSSING. Mating together birds that are not related or of a different colour.

PIED. A bird with its dark colour irregularly broken with light areas.

RECESSIVE. A colour that when crossed with a Normal has no visual effect on the colour of the young produced.

SADDLE. The area of the upper back.

SEX-LINKED. A colour character that is carried on the sex determining chromosome pair.

SINGLE CHARACTER. A bird that has a colour character on only one of its chromosome pair.

SPLIT. A term used to indicate that a bird of one colour carries another colour character in its genetical make-up.

THEORETICAL EXPECTATIONS. The calculated results according to Mendel's Laws from the crossing of two colours.

WILD TYPE. The form of the species that is found in the wild.

WING BUTTS. The bend of the wings when lying close to the body.

INDEX